JUSTICE FOR ALL

Issues in Political Philosophy

Edited by
Steven P. Scalet

Series in Philosophy, Politics and Law
Global Publications, Binghamton University
Binghamton, New York
2002

SERIES IN PHILOSOPHY, POLITICS AND LAW
Editor in Chief: Steven P. Scalet
Managing Editor: Shalahudin Kafrawi

Library of Congress Cataloging-in-Publication Data:

ISBN 1-58684-241-2

Cover photograph by Steven P. Scalet.
Cover design by Shalahudin Kafrawi.

Published by:
Global Publications, Binghamton University
State University of New York
Binghamton, New York, USA 13902-6000
Phone: (607) 777-4495 Fax: (607) 777-6132
E-mail: info@globalpublicationspress.com
http://globalpublicationspress.com

INTRODUCTION

Five hours into the conference, the audience of thirty students and faculty reached another five minute break: a few people exited, four or five entered, small discussions arose about the room, and then silence. The last speaker of the evening, Thomas Wynn, strode to the lectern and delivered his fifteen-minute presentation. The three judging panelists sat politely and listened to his brisk delivery about modeling a legal right. A moment for applause and then less than five seconds later, the panelists hammered away for half an hour with their questions and positions as Mr. Wynn retorted, rebuffed, and held on.

So went the Honors Conference that was the cornerstone for this publication. Six undergraduate honors students delivered philosophy papers during this six-hour conference on April 29, 2002, at Binghamton University in Binghamton, New York. The Honors Conference was the result of four months of work for these students and brought to focus their four years of philosophy study through the writing and defense of an independent senior thesis. Each of the six presentations that Monday created its own high energy and charged exchanges. The collection of papers in this volume derives from that conference.

Can we offer undergraduate students a graduate-level and professional experience within the undergraduate curriculum? This conference and publication address that challenge.

Let top students apply for admission into a competitive honors program; inform them from the outset that a panel of academics will examine and judge their presentations in front of a general audience; direct the writing process, encourage regular debates among the students, and coach them on delivering a scholarly paper. These were the basic ingredients for meeting that challenge.

Binghamton University has over 100 philosophy majors and over 350 majors in the related interdisciplinary Program in Philosophy, Politics and Law (PPL). PPL includes core courses in philosophy and complimentary courses in history, political science, economics, and other humanities and social sciences. These are strong liberal arts majors, and the Honors Program is part of creating the personal attention that is the hallmark of small liberal arts colleges. The Honors Program works primarily by self-selection: the most motivated and interested students gravitate to the program by responding to invitations and advertisements, or through recommendations from other faculty. From hundreds of majors comes this small group of highly capable and highly motivated students.

As a faculty member, the hard work of mentoring graduate students is gratifying, and pursuing research and writing is a life-long enrichment. But the focus on undergraduates is a fundamental mission. These students debated with each other as peers in small circles and in front of a general audience, delivered papers, and published their ideas. These are the activities that professors pursue, and it was gratifying to witness them have that experience. As undergraduates they got a taste of the excitement and power of ideas, and the value of sustaining communities based on intellectual exchange and debate. The energy was exhilarating.

Each of the papers is an original work by the student author, both in conception and development. The role of the faculty advisors was to guide the writing process with a light hand (or the occasional firm suggestion). Each paper has its own abstract at the beginning of each article, so I will not summarize the contributions here.

This book is the first volume in the *Series in Philosophy, Politics and Law*, published through Global Publications, Inc. Topics may range over any area of general philosophy, as well as political philosophy and legal philosophy. The title of the series recognizes the role of Binghamton University's PPL Program as the origination of the series. The current volume, *Justice for All: Essays in Political Philosophy*, is so-named because all the papers in this volume focus on concerns of justice within contemporary political philosophy.

I wish to thank Binghamton alumnus Owen C. Pell, Esq. '80, whose financial contributions made possible the organization of these proceedings. Mr. Pell has devoted his energy and enthusiasm to support liberal arts education within a public institution – the State University of New York at Binghamton. He has been a frequent guest lecturer to the classroom over the years. His captivating speaking style and his command over a vast range of issues in law and legal philosophy make him a favorite among students. It is an honor to give him tribute.

I am also grateful to Professor John Arthur, Director of the Program in Philosophy, Politics and Law. Professor Arthur's work over the last decade has created the vibrancy and success of the PPL Program which has grown from a few dozens majors to over 350 majors under his tenure. I would also like to thank Professors Bat-Ami Bar On, Christopher Knapp and Max Pensky for their work as faculty advisors. Finally, I wish to thank Professor Tony Preus for serving as a panelist (alongside Professor Arthur and Mr. Pell), and Shalahudin Kafrawi for his editorial assistance in creating this publication.

I extend a special gratitude and admiration to Professor Michael Roth at Franklin and Marshall College in Lancaster, Pennsylvania.* He was my undergraduate advisor ten years ago and supervised my senior thesis on Aristotle's ethics. More than anyone else, he gave to me the inspiration that I hope will pass on to others.

May the spirit of philosophical inquiry live among people of all ages and at all times.

Steven P. Scalet
Director, 3/2 Graduate Program in Philosophy, Politics and Law
Assistant Professor, Philosophy and Economics

* Professor Roth died unexpectedly prior to the final proofs for this publication. Professor Roth truly was a remarkable and passionate teacher. For over thirty years he mentored and influenced generations of philosophy students. I dedicate this volume in his memory.

CONTENTS

JUSTICE FOR ALL

Issues in Political Philosophy

Abstract

Safety is extremely important, and any just society must value it. Safety requires at least subsistence because human life is valuable. Our society is rightfully committed to keeping people safe. I argue, by developing an analogy, that if it is right to attempt to rescue those trapped in a fire, regardless of who is responsible for the fire, then we should provide for subsistence, regardless of responsibility or fault.

In this paper, I will explain the analogy between fire protection and providing subsistence. There is no difference, in principle, between saving someone trapped in a burning building and saving someone from starvation. I will define safety, and explain why it is important. Finally, I argue that the government is the best entity to provide safety for two reasons. First, the government is the only entity that can provide safety. Second, it is part of the government's purpose to provide safety.

SAFETY FIRST

Justifying Guaranteed Subsistence Regardless of Responsibility

Adam Ross

1. Introduction

Safety is extremely important, and any just society must value it. Safety requires at least subsistence because human life is valuable. Our society is rightfully committed to keeping people safe. I argue, by developing an analogy, that if it is right to attempt to rescue those trapped in a fire, regardless of who is responsible for the fire, then we should provide for subsistence, regardless of responsibility or fault.

In this paper, I will explain the analogy between fire protection and providing subsistence. There is no difference, in principle, between saving someone trapped in a burning building and saving someone from starvation. I will define safety and explain why it is important.

Finally, I will argue that the government is the best entity to provide safety for two reasons. First, the government is the only entity that can provide safety. Second, it is part of the government's purpose to provide safety.

This is an ethical argument, and although I will suggest policy implications that follow from it, I will not attempt to explain if, or how, the government could practically implement these policies. Also, one could make an argument that safety requires giving people more than subsistence, but I will not address that issue here.

2. A Hypothetical Example

Imagine a fire truck speeding toward a burning building. The fire is in the middle of a field, and puts no other property or lives in danger. The firefighters find a family trapped in the building. Now imagine the ladder extending from the truck to the family trapped in the building, and the firefighter asking, "Before I save you, could you tell me if you are responsible for this fire through negligence or arson? If you are, I am not going to save you." There seems to be something very wrong with this. The focus is wrongly on responsibility and not safety. It seems right that society should save people from a burning building, or most crises, when their lives are in jeopardy, regardless of whether they are responsible for the danger.

This analogy applies to most serious dangers. Is it wrong for the government to not attempt to rescue a person in danger because they were responsible for the danger? I argue that it does not matter who is at fault, or who is responsible for the crisis. If we are committed to saving those in a burning building regardless of fault, then we should be committed to saving those who are in life threatening danger regardless of who is responsible for that danger. In this case, the fire is analogous to a lack of subsistence because both situations are life-threatening dangers, and in both cases, even if those in need caused the danger, they do not deserve to die.

Subsistence usually means that people have enough resources to "remain in existence" or "to be supported or to live" (Williams 1991: 908). I will stay with that definition with one addition for now. Providing people with subsistence means providing them with enough to survive and remain intact in the best reasonable health. This may be hopelessly subjective because people require different amounts of subsistence to survive. I will not, however, address that issue. Later, I will provide a more specific list of what subsistence requires. For now, only a general understanding is necessary. Remember, my main argument is for government provided subsistence in the name of safety.

3. What is Safety, and Why is it Important?

In this section I will define safety and explain why it is important. In the next section I will apply this to justify the intuition that it is right to save people from danger regardless of responsibility. In the last sections, I will talk about possible policy implications and argue that the government is the proper entity to provide safety.

Safety is protection from danger. This kind of danger could put a person's physical, emotional, or mental health at risk to debilitating injury. By debilitating injury, I mean eliminating any reasonable chance at being able to develop or use one's capacities in some valuable way. This means that the person in danger must have already had a reasonable chance at developing or using her capacities, and this danger could jeopardize that. The entity that is responsible for keeping people safe is not responsible for creating opportunities or preserving them. It is only responsible for providing a reasonable amount of help in times of crisis. Life threatening danger clearly counts as debilitating. One can think of safety as a worthy goal that society ought to achieve.

When the danger is severe enough (when it could interfere with an individual's ability to develop or use her capacities in some meaningful way) society creates institutions to reduce or eliminate the danger. (For now I will assume that the government should be the entity to provide safety. I will argue for this in section six.)

There is a distinction between safety and rights protection (or security), although one could imagine a right to be safe. One usually thinks of rights of security as protections from injury caused by others. This is a part of safety, but it does not capture the whole idea. Safety is more robust than security. It includes protections against those harms that are self-inflicted and caused by bad luck. Safety is also broader in the sense that it is a preventative as well as a remedial goal. It requires that people be helped in certain kinds of danger, and if possible to stop the dangerous situations from taking place. Most think of safety as a privilege or benefit of living in civil society rather than a right. Though there is a distinction between safety and rights of security, it is one of degree. Rights are those safeties society deems so important that they are fundamental to the bare minimum adequate life. In this paper I use an expansive definition of safety. What one usually thinks of as safety in a political sense is merely security.

A working definition of what constitutes an adequate life is necessary to explain why safety is so important. My definition of adequate has two aspects and is limited to modern liberal societies. The following two criteria are necessary to live an adequate life, but may not be sufficient. First, the possibility exists for people to live an adequate life when they are given some choice as to how to develop their capacities in a meaningful way. One determines what is valuable or meaningful by society's condemning that which it does not deem valuable through societal norms and laws. Second, people must also have the opportunity to do something meaningful. If they are dead or starving (this does not include those who choose to die or starve) they will not be able to develop, use, or continue developing their capacities in some meaningful way.

I will provide a concrete example to explain what qualifies as an adequate life. Take Jane for example, who is an American citizen. Jane wants to be a doctor, but does not do well on the MCAT. Because of this, no medical school admits her. Just because she did not achieve this valuable goal does not mean she cannot live an adequate life. She can still choose many other worthy goals. Jane can still be a dentist, a teacher or a sanitation worker. Safety does not require society to provide Jane with a medical education. The entity responsible for keeping people safe is not responsible for creating the choice or chance per se, but instead must provide the background conditions that make an adequate life a possibility for all. There is a minimal amount of safety required as a background condition. Subsistence is part of the safety that is necessary.

Now, imagine that Jane is trapped in a burning building. If she dies in the fire she will not have the opportunity to do, or continue to do, something valuable, with her life. Both Jane and society will have lost something of great value.

It is now clearer why safety is important. When society is protecting life, not property, safety is an end in itself. With no sense of safety it would be hard to carry on routine activities. Pursuing a valuable goal is impossible without at least some safety. Imagine being in a burning building all the time. People would be so preoccupied with staying alive that nothing else would matter. One can put this in terms of social contract theory. People came out of the state of nature because there was no security (enforced scheme of rights) and because there was no safety.

Eduardo Maynez, in "Justice and Legal Security," claims that security (his argument could be extended to safety) has only instrumental value (Maynez 1949: 500). Safety's value flows from what it keeps safe. It is the thing kept safe, not safety, that is truly valued. This does not hold true when the object of safety is the preservation of human life. Safety's value may flow from the value of human life, at least in the sense that we each value our own lives. When the protected thing is so important it is inconceivable to want to live without it, keeping that thing safe becomes an end in itself. Whether one recognizes that safety is an end in itself is not as important as realizing that safety is extremely valuable to us. Whether it is because we need safety to live a valuable life or that we value our lives themselves, safety is important.

4. Justifying My Intuition

Now that I have defined safety and we understand why safety is important, we can analyze the fire analogy with new vocabulary. It is right that the government should save people from the burning building because it should keep people safe. Safety is an important goal that society must achieve for people to have the possibility of doing something meaningful with their lives. Safety is important in a more basic sense because people value their own lives and, through empathy, can realize that other's lives matter too. Recall the image of Jane trapped in a burning building. If Jane dies in that fire, her death eliminates the possibility of her developing or using her capacities in some meaningful way. Similarly, if Jane dies of starvation or some easily curable disease, she loses the same possibility.

When people are in danger that could put the possibility of their living an adequate life in jeopardy (trapped in a burning building), society should attempt to help them. There are several reasons society should attempt to rescue Jane unconditionally. First, human life is valuable, at least in the sense that people usually value their own lives. It is senseless and wasteful to let potential contributors die needlessly in a fire. Perhaps Jane was a scientist, an artist, or a mother. Perhaps she was none of these things, but had the potential to do something valuable.

Second, no one wants to die in a fire. No one wants to let their loved ones die either. Because we would want unconditional protection for ourselves and loved ones, we are able to see why it is valuable to give it to others. At least we realize it is necessary to give it to others within our society if we really want it for ourselves. Also, humans have the ability to empathize. We can imagine what it would be like for Jane, trapped in the burning building, and because we would not want to die that way, it is reasonable to believe that Jane would not want to either. Similarly, few, if any, want to die of starvation or freeze to death. When safety is jeopardized and society is able, it seems almost cruel not to help.

Third, safety is an important goal. Safety is obviously served better by attempting to rescue Jane in the fire, rather than leaving her to die. In the same respect, safety is served better by feeding Jane if she is starving to death. Society satisfies safety better by providing subsistence. When trapped in a fire, our focus should be on safety and not responsibility. Responsibility is part of keeping people safe, but is not more important than safety.

One could consider responsibility a value that serves the end of safety. Perhaps responsible behavior should be encouraged in every situation, but there is no just society that should value responsibility over safety. Encouraging responsibility is encouraging people to act in ways that keep themselves and society safe. The goal, however, is safety, and not responsibility. Encouraging responsible behavior is one way to keep people safe, but sometimes social norms and laws that are in place for this purpose fail, and when they do, society should step in. Even the most responsible people make mistakes and have accidents. Thinking responsibility is more important than safety is a mistake that one makes when one does not realize that part of the point of responsibility is to keep individuals, and society as a whole, safe.

Even in a society that provides subsistence, there is incentive to take responsibility for yourself without having to threaten to take safety away. To use the fire example, most people do not want their house to burn down. People have smoke detectors and fire extinguishers even though they know society has guaranteed a rescue attempt. Perhaps the prospect of losing your house is enough incentive to take responsibility for fire safety. The idea that although society guarantees a rescue attempt, but does not guarantee success, is certainly enough. (This last sentence does not really apply to subsistence.)

People may be more responsible for fire safety if they are not guaranteed an unconditional rescue attempt, but at what cost? Many would become so preoccupied with keeping their house safe it would interfere with their living a normal life. In the same respect, most people do not want to live at the bare minimum of subsistence and suffer the negative social and psychological effects of being unemployed. This will be enough incentive to keep most, if not all, people working, and ease the burden of those who are out of work because of bad luck, stupidity, or laziness.

Responsibility comes into play when considering luxury items. Luxury items are things that one can live without. For example, it seems wrong to send a firefighter into a burning building to get a painting, no matter how valuable it may be. This may be reflective of society's understanding that there is something invaluable about human life. It may, however, just be reflective of people's caring about themselves and valuing their own lives. In valuing their own lives, they want unconditional protection and must be willing to give it to others to create that protection for themselves.

Society is therefore right to save people in a burning building regardless of whether they are responsible for the fire. In a similar respect society is right to provide subsistence. What are the relevant similarities between the fire and a lack of subsistence that makes the analogy applicable? First, in both situations, even if Jane's irresponsible behavior causes the fire or lack of subsistence, she does not deserve to die because of her irresponsibility. Our society has not condoned employing the death penalty to punish far worse crimes than negligence. This is why it seems cruel and unfair to let her die.

I believe this first reason is extremely persuasive. Our society values each individual life. Human life has some inherent value that seems to be independent of our actions. This value is hard to define or pin down, but our society seems to be committed to respecting individual worth. This is another reason why we save people trapped in fires. They have worth that we must preserve. This reason applies directly to feeding the starving. We provide subsistence to preserve this value.

Second, there is at least a chance that helping the person would successfully keep them safe. Third, whether Jane is trapped in a burning building or lacks subsistence, she does not want to be in that situation, and is desperate to get out of it. Fourth, they are both life-threatening dangers.

Clearly, both the fire and lacking subsistence are dangers that could cause fatal or debilitating injury. If one is so poor that she cannot get enough food, shelter or basic medical care, her condition can lead to a serious injury. Society should protect citizens by keeping them safe enough to live without fear of death or incapacitation due to lack of subsistence. That kind of fear interferes with a person's ability to live an adequate life, pursue her own ends, and fully develop as a human being.

One could object that a person is poor because she is lazy or stupid. If one does not take responsibility for her actions, why should society protect her? There are many instances where a poor person is in her situation because of undeserved inequalities and bad luck. Lacking intellect is neither a crime nor a choice. People cannot choose their natural limitations any more than they can choose who their parents are. One cannot expect a five year old to take responsibility for her food intake when her parents are too poor to feed her. Further, even when people are responsible for their own grave danger, society should help for safety's sake.

Society should seek to limit and rectify injuries it causes, directly or indirectly, through institutions that it endorses. If being poor constitutes danger caused by some institution, then the government should eliminate that danger. Sometimes people's economic disadvantage is their own fault. In these cases, when people are in dire need, as in the case of a family in a burning building, society should still help. While society should hold people accountable for their mistakes, economic mistakes do not warrant a death sentence. After all, most think it is inhumane to let rapists and bank robbers starve, so why should we let the irresponsible starve?

Society should keep us safe even when it is not the entity causing the harm. We want the government to provide us with police and fire protection even if they had nothing to do with the danger being caused by criminals or fires. What is at stake is too precious to go unprotected, and the government is the only entity that can keep us safe.

One could raise five objections. First, one could argue that there are some relevant differences between the burning building and lacking subsistence. Second, one could claim that some luxury items are necessary to live an adequate life. Third, one could claim that if subsistence were provided there are many who would not work and become drains on society. Fourth, one could argue that freedom is more important than safety and these goals conflict. Finally, one could claim that my argument requires that I personify society.

One point someone may find wrong with the hypothetical is that the government does not stop the fire from happening, they just help once the fire happens. Providing people with subsistence would be equivalent to stopping the fire before it starts. The government, however, does try to stop the fire before it starts. It legislates building code laws that minimize the risk of fires, and some local governments require smoke detectors and fire extinguishers. These laws are attempts on the part of the government to limit the risk of permanent, debilitating injury from fires by helping stop them before they start or get out of control. In principle, there is no real difference here. Society is keeping individuals safe by assisting them in a crisis. Second, in both situations, the fire and lack of subsistence, the government is stopping the danger from causing permanent, debilitating injury.

One can object to the hypothetical by pointing out that a fire is a more immediate danger than starvation. When one is about to be burned alive every second counts, and it is better to save her first and ask questions later. This is not so with starvation. No one dies instantly of malnourishment. In theory, it could be determined who is at fault for the starving person's situation before any permanent damage is done. Perhaps if they are not responsible we should help them, but if they are, we should not. This is ludicrous. Not helping those who are starving to death because they were irresponsible is analogous to putting Jane back into the burning building if, after we save her, we determine she was responsible for the fire.

There are two ways of interpreting fault in this situation. There is fault through negligence and fault through intentional action. If a family member started the fire (or is starving) through negligence, society should still attempt to rescue the family. Does a mistake warrant a death sentence? In our legal system, even gross negligence is not a capital crime. The case for safety is even more compelling for those who are at fault by intentionally starving themselves. This unusual situation does happen. Society looks upon anorexia as a disease to cure. Our society provides suicidal people with medical help, and it should.

One could next object by claiming that the fire is transitory. It is easy to define when a fire starts and stops, and easy to assess when the government should help. It is much harder to define when someone is starving or lacking subsistence. First, it is not as easy as one may think to point out when a fire starts and stops. Imagine a brush fire that burns for months at a time. Second, it is not so easy to say when the government should begin to help. There are several situations that are not life threatening where the government would stop a fire. Imagine a garbage can in a public park that is on fire. Perhaps a small fire in an office, school or private home that individuals can easily put out. Often the fire department is called to make sure the fire is out. Although it is not always easy to define when a fire starts and stops, or when the government should be called to help, when there is an interest in saving human life the government should help.

Most of the time, factors outside of the control of the suffering people cause the fire or lack of subsistence. When bad luck causes a fire, people expect that the government will protect them through the fire department. If society is committed to safety then people should rightfully expect society to feed them when they are starving to death. In principle, there is no difference between the danger of dying in a fire and the danger of dying from starvation.

Moving to the second objection, there may be some luxury items that Jane needs to live an adequate life, but no luxury item is necessary for everyone to live an adequate life. One thing, however, is clear. If people do not have enough to subsist then it is impossible for them to live an adequate life, because they will not live at all.

One can object that providing subsistence will create a society of beach bums, who are content with subsistence and nothing more. Just like the fire, there is personal incentive to stop the danger. Few would ever desire to get to a point where subsistence would have to be provided. There will still be incentive to work. I doubt the bare minimum would be enough for most people. In a society as materialistic as this one, I find it hard to believe that people would be willing to settle for plain oatmeal when they could work and get sugared oatmeal or oatmeal with raisins. There is more value in working than just gaining luxury items, although this will be part of people's motivation to work. People will not want to suffer negative treatment from society that comes along with being unemployed. Self-esteem and the pride that come along with earning a salary and being 'responsible' are important reasons for people to work. Even with motivation to work, some would not, if society provided subsistence. I do not think they would constitute a large enough portion of society to be harmful. Society should still feed these people. The punishment for laziness should not be death.

Another strong objection to the idea that society should provide people with safety is that safety is in conflict with freedom, and freedom is more important. Safety and freedom are both goals our society is, and should be, deeply committed to satisfying. Although freedom and safety are goals that sometimes clash, they are not always in conflict. In fact, in many situations each goal helps foster the other. It is only when safety or freedom become too encompassing that they interfere with the other. To maximize freedom would be to live without safety or order. There is always a danger of the government going too far to keep people safe because we need a certain amount of freedom to live an adequate life. We would never want to maximize either of these goals, but instead, find the right balance.

At what point does safety impinge on freedom, and which goal is more important? Which value is more important varies because of specific situations in each society. During peacetime, in a liberal society, freedom has the balance. In peacetime, society should provide the maximum amount of freedom while still providing the minimum amount of safety. During wartime, the answer is not so clear.

Even if freedom is generally more important than safety, it does not mean that it is more important than safety in every situation or that safety is unimportant. It may suggest different policy implications. For instance, people should be allowed to refuse safety when their freedom is at stake. I do not believe that this is something in opposition to my argument that society should provide people with subsistence for safety's sake. Because freedom is of no use to those who are starving to death, in situations where subsistence is in question, safety has the balance. "It is true that to offer political rights, or safeguards against intervention by the state, to men who are half-naked, illiterate, underfed, and diseased is to mock their condition; they need medical help or education before they can understand, or make use of, an increase in their freedom" (Berlin1964: 124).

Lastly, some could claim that for my argument to work I must personify society. Society cannot have goals. People have goals. Society does not value safety; people do. If society cannot have goals or values, then why should the government promote these goals?

In a democracy, the government should promote safety because people want someone to keep them safe. All we need for the government to promote safety is the fact that people want it provided. People only need to value their own lives. To a certain extent though, I believe that it is not wrong to personify a society. The smaller and more homogeneous the society the easier and more accurate it is to do. A country shares a history and to some extent a culture. It is not unusual, therefore, for many in a society to share goals and common experiences. Personification is not necessary, however, because individuals value safety and human life.

Society should therefore provide at least subsistence for safety's sake. If one is committed to the idea that saving those in a fire is a good thing that we should want society to do regardless of whether the victims are responsible for the fire, then we are committed to the idea that we must feed the starving, clothe the naked, and house the homeless regardless of responsibility. Other levels of equality may require the display of responsible choices, but people should not suffer or die because they were irresponsible. Sometimes this happens. Some people who contracted the HIV virus were irresponsible in their sexual or drug habits. Do they then deserve to die? If the government had a cure, would it be justified in withholding it from those with AIDS who were irresponsible? I think not.

5. Policy Implications

So what policy implications stem from these ideas? First, the government should provide all those within the borders of a society with safety. This at least includes guaranteeing subsistence, police and fire protection, and protection from invasion. Society should not be responsible for replacing any luxury item that is lost because of irresponsible behavior, but irresponsible behavior is not enough to warrant a death sentence.

Let us revisit Jane trapped in the building. We should save Jane whether or not she is a citizen. If Jane is a legal resident alien, we should save her from the burning building. Jane is trying to be a part of our society. She is making an effort to learn our laws and customs, and living with the same burdens that citizens do. She is human and her life has value.

There are some that would object to these policies. Although philosophical writings on safety are scarce, there is a long line of economic writings on the cost of saving lives. The classic interpretation claims that society should only save someone's life if it would improve the aggregate welfare. The aggregate welfare is improved by saving someone's life if it would cost society less to save that life than the loss society would suffer if the person died. Part of this calculation includes figuring out how much someone is worth, and people are worth vastly different amounts depending on age, quality of life, earning potential, skill, etc. (Oi 1995: 67). Under this interpretation, society should not always attempt to save everyone it could. Researchers should provide a cost benefit analysis on Jane when she is in danger and from this, they should decide whether she should be saved. If her life is worth less than the price it would cost to save her, society should not attempt a rescue.

This is a strong objection to the idea that society should unconditionally try to keep people safe. This is just one more example why the maximization of aggregate welfare should not be the focus when determining whether to save someone's life. For example, imagine Jane is a poor, old woman who has no living relatives, is retired, and is not in very good health. Her life would not be worth much in dollars, and perhaps if trapped in a burning building, it would cost more to save her than the loss her death would cause. According to the above analysis, we should let Jane die. Something seems very wrong about this. It relates to a critique of using welfare as a judge of ethics (utilitarianism).

There are three ways to phrase this critique. First, the government violated Jane's rights by not saving her. To believe this, one would have to believe in rights. To believe in rights one must believe that human beings have intrinsic worth. These terms are unclear and extremely hard to define, but there seems to be something right about this.

Second, there is something about Jane being human that makes her life worth something that one cannot express in dollars. There is something about this that does not respect Jane as an individual (Rawls 1999: 294-5). This also relates to the idea that people have intrinsic worth. This is not to say that the safety of one is more important than the safety of many, but that no one person's safety is ethically more important than any other single person's safety.

Third, society has decided to make safety a goal that, in certain cases, outweighs maximization of the aggregate welfare. While utilitarian goals are legitimate, they are often outweighed by other goals deemed more important by society. Society may have made safety a goal because it wanted to respect people's rights, inherent worth, or equality, but this was not necessary. One of the advantages to grounding justifications in goals is that one does not have to be committed to abstract ideas like rights and inherent worth. People only have to realize that they want to be treated a certain way or have certain conditions in society be met, and for that to happen they must be willing for everyone else to enjoy the same benefits.

Similarly, this theory overcomes a theoretical objection to most liberal egalitarian theories (theories that primarily value liberty and equality and see a generally robust role for government as compared to classic liberals). Along with desert, egalitarians often (if only indirectly) appeal to fairness. Their focus usually is to eliminate undeserved inequalities or envy. These undeserved inequalities in resources are unfair and/or unjust. Arguments for equality can only appeal to fairness if we recognize that people matter equally. There is, however, an element of circular logic. Equality is justified by fairness, but fairness only matters if people are equal. This is overcome by grounding the justification of economic equality in values other than fairness.

By justifying government provided subsistence through an appeal to safety, one can avoid grounding the justification in equal concern for citizens, although that should probably be part of the justification. In this way, it overcomes the circular logic trap of fairness. Because providing subsistence promotes safety, it is justified and we do not need to show that people are equal, just that they value safety. In this way, we can stop the regression. Safety matters regardless of whether people are equal. Safety matters because it is necessary to lead an adequate life. This would matter to the most and least important (assuming people are unequal).

6. Government is the Proper Entity to Provide Safety

I argue that the government is the right entity to provide safety partly because they are the only entity that can achieve this goal. Just because the government is the only entity that can keep us safe, however, does not mean the government is the right entity to do this. Of course, we already know that society should keep people safe, so it may come down to what part of society is the best provider of safety. For now, the government can do this best. If some other institution would provide safety as well or better, should we let them? More importantly, some would object that it is not the government's place to provide people with safety.

Before I defend the view that the government should provide safety, I must be more specific about exactly what safety requires the government to provide. The government must provide safety in a very limited sense. The government should provide all the safety required as a background condition for creating the possibility for everyone to live an adequate life. This does not mean that the government, or anyone but the individual, is responsible for actually achieving personal goals. Nor does it imply that the government should create opportunities for people. It means the government should foster background conditions that will create the potential for opportunity. Opportunities must be able to exist in society. This means two things. First, people need to be free to make choices about what ends they most value. Second, people need to be safe enough to make well thought out decisions.

What background conditions are necessary to create the possibility to live an adequate life? People need to be free, safe, educated, and treated equally. I am not sure that this list is exhaustive, and what each of these things implies is heavily debated, but at least one thing is certain. If the government does not guarantee subsistence, it will not meet the background conditions in the following ways. First, those people who are starving or homeless will be severely hindered in pursuing an adequate life. Second, if people are struggling to pay the bills, they are not free enough to pursue their ends. Safety, therefore, is a necessary background condition to opportunity.

What exactly does 'starving' or 'homeless' mean? These terms are vague. Specifically, what is the government required to provide? There are several aspects to subsistence. First, people must have enough nutrition. 'Enough nutrition' means that people are not malnourished or unhealthy as defined by medical standards.

Second, people must have adequate shelter. This does not imply that the government should provide people with real property or that ownership is necessary. Adequate shelter means several things. First, it means some permanent structure that protects against the elements and provides the following modern conveniences: running water and heat. Second, it must provide an address that one can use on a job application. This shelter does not have to be limited to one person or family, but I have something more than a homeless shelter in mind.

Third, people must have adequate clothing for subsistence to be satisfied. This means more than just rags or coverings. People should have clothes they can work in, whether this means a suit or overalls. They do not need designer clothing, but at least what is necessary for people to be employable.

Fourth, and perhaps most controversial, subsistence requires universal medical care. This would have to include preventative, as well as repairing measures. Annual physicals, prescribed medication, and recommended surgery all must be included. Although this is the most controversial, it is the most similar to being trapped in a burning building. Usually, bad luck or irresponsible behavior causes the fire or sickness.

One can object that this is a lot more than just saving a person's life. When trapped in a fire, the government only saves the person's life. This relates to the objection that the government does not stop the fire before it starts. One must remember that safety is, in part, a preventative goal. Examples of this include governments legislating building codes that reduce the risk of fires, or requiring by law that people have smoke detectors and fire extinguishers in their home.

The government is the only entity capable of providing an adequate amount of safety, and because safety needs to be provided, it is the best entity to do it. It is the only entity with enough power to achieve the goal, and government can achieve the goal quicker than any other entity. It is precisely the government's place to provide for safety, but only those safeties that are required to have the opportunity to live a good life.

Safety is a public good. It is non-depleteable because one person's use of it will not reduce the amount for another person, and non-rival because no one is excluded from it. The government is the most efficient provider of this public good because it is the only entity in society that can provide it in a sufficient amount to be effective. The government is unique in its ability to tax and spend, and can compel individuals to help provide for the public good.

What competition does the government have? One could argue that the market, individuals, or the church, should provide people with this good. All of these possibilities fail for different reasons. Where they fail, the government succeeds.

Next to the government, the most plausible candidate for providing safety is the market. There are many markets for safety now. Home security systems are an example of this. A flaw with markets is especially apparent where safety is concerned. Markets are excellent for producing a good, and for distributing goods to those who most want them. They are not, however, so great at distributing goods to those who most need them. Safety (especially subsistence) is a needed good. If the market were to provide for safety, it would invariably leave out the poorest people. If they do not have enough money to pay for food, then they do not have enough money to pay for safety. Because they are the people who lack subsistence, letting the market provide it seems to defeat the purpose.

The government would be able to produce safety at least as well as the market, and be a better distributor of safety because who could afford safety would not be a determining factor in whom it provides with safety. A government has the ability to tax and spend, and can use this ability to produce a public good. Markets can, and perhaps should, produce some public goods. Other public goods are so important that they are necessary to respect the inherent worth of people, and everyone should benefit from them. Safety is in the latter category. When this is the case, the government is the best provider.

Neither the individual, nor the small groups of individuals organized as charitable entities are able to achieve the goal of safety. If individuals are responsible for providing safety for others after them, it will create the classic problems of free riding and assurance associated with public goods.

Social norms of responsibility whose purpose is to encourage safe behavior do not always work. In this situation, if individuals are responsible for providing safety, they will not be able to provide a large enough quantity of this public good. Individuals are bad providers of public goods because they are caught in a prisoner's type dilemma. Although it would be better for everyone if individuals voluntarily contributed to create the public good of safety, it is in everyone's own best interest to keep their money. If anyone contributes, she will create the public good that everyone else will enjoy. Those who did not contribute get to keep what they originally had and enjoy the public good. Either this 'free-rider' problem will assure that the people will not create the public good, or they will not create it in a large enough quantity to be effective. People will not contribute unless they are assured everyone else will. The government can accomplish this through taxation.

There are some, like Ellickson, who would object that individuals would create public goods on their own. This may be true when dealing with small amounts of people where few resources are at stake. When one considers the enormous amount of resources involved in keeping people safe, it seems unlikely that individuals would be able to accomplish the task. Even if they were able to accomplish the task, it seems unlikely they would be willing to devote enough of their resources unless they were assured others would too.

Take, for example, a neighborhood watch group that helps produce a higher level of the public good of safety. Individuals definitely could provide some protection by organizing small groups to patrol their streets. This may even be enough for a rural town, but it does not seem like an effective neighborhood watch could be established that would produce enough safety for New York City. The government is the only entity capable of keeping us safe because it has far more resources at its disposal than individuals.

R.F. Swift claims that the church should be responsible for providing safety through charity, social norms and spiritual salvation (Swift 1924: 362). Although I doubt the government can or should provide spiritual safety, I doubt even more highly that the church could provide adequate protection against fire or starvation. They do not have the means. Also, to allow the church to take over a traditional governmental role would violate the constitutional principle of separation of church and state, and all the negatives associated with it.

The government is the best provider of safety. The government is also responsible for safety, not only because it is the only entity that can provide it, but because it is the right entity to provide it. It is one of the primary purposes of government to keep us safe. This is one of the government's main functions. In modern liberal societies, the whole point of living under a government is to be as free as possible and still be safe. Would anyone come out of a state of nature, where there is maximal freedom, if there was no guarantee of safety under the rule of a government?

Several types of protections are intertwined with the purpose of government. Protection from invasion, limited property rights, and police and fire protection are included in this category. The list should also include protection from starvation, the elements, and curable disease. Societies that are able to provide all of these protections should. Governments that cannot provide these protections may not be legitimate. If a country could not provide protection from invasion or property rights violations, it would have its legitimacy questioned. In the same respect, if the government cannot keep people free and safe, it is treating its citizens as less than human and is illegitimate.

Some may object to the idea that it is part of the government's purpose to keep us safe. They could claim that it is paternalistic in the sense that it transforms the government into some benevolent parental figure who keeps us safe out of general concern. In doing this I transform the government into something it is not. Moreover, although it may be nice to have an extra parent looking out for us, we certainly do not need a new dad or mom telling us what to do.

On the surface this seems valid, but one must remember that no one in society needs to care about anyone else to value safety. All that matters is that people value their own lives. If they do, they should value, and therefore want society to provide them with at least some safety. In a democracy, the Government should create safety because people are selfish and want it for themselves. In this situation, the provider of safety (government) is doing its job and carrying out the will of the people. The government is indifferent to each individual person. I will concede that it does not have to be this way, and I do not believe this would be the best way to interpret government provided safety. I do not claim that governments that provide safety cannot be paternalistic, just that they do not need to be paternalistic to provide safety. If paternalism is something a society condemns, then the government could still provide safety without the idea of a benevolent father figure.

One could claim that it is not the proper place of the government to keep people safe. They might say that it should be the job of markets, individuals, or some combination.

The market allows people to exercise their freedom in ways that will hopefully lead to mutually beneficial exchange. It seems like the market is an inherently risky institution. Even insurance is risky, if one can afford it. There are never any guarantees an investment will make a profit. At most, one could argue that the market provides certain kinds of economic freedoms, but to make the claim that the market's purpose is to provide safety to individuals seems contradictory. The market's capacities seem too limited in scope to handle safety.

One could then object that the burden of keeping people safe is on the individual through being responsible. Even the most responsible people's lives are put in danger sometimes. When that happens, as we now see, the government should help regardless of fault.

Is it part of the purpose of being an individual to be safe, or promote safety? Perhaps, but it is not part of the purpose of being an individual to provide safety for everyone else. Perhaps one could argue that part of the purpose of being a parent is to keep your children safe, but not society. To put the responsibility of keeping everyone safe on the individual would be too burdensome, and some of the value of individuality would be lost. One of the reasons we value individuality is because we value being able to develop in a meaningful way we choose. This choice is important to us. If an individual were always worried about having to keep everyone else safe, it would limit her ability to develop, and thus limit the value of her choosing.

6. Conclusion

I will conclude by bringing up a final concern, and restating my main argument. My main argument in this paper applies to citizens and resident aliens of a particular country. But how far does our commitment to safety go? If Jane is an illegal alien trapped in a fire, should she be saved? If the United States Government could, should it be required to save Jane from a burning building if she was a Chinese citizen living in Hong Kong? Would the United States government be ethically committed to provide a third world country's citizens with subsistence? Although an argument based on safety could be part of the justification for helping illegal aliens and people in other countries, it is not enough. There are other goals and values that one must consider.

Part of the reason we value safety is because modern Western liberals value the individual and human life. If this justification for keeping people safe is persuasive then perhaps, this is enough to justify helping illegal aliens and people in other countries. After all, they are just as human as we are.

We must not forget, however, that there is a sense of community within a country that is fostered by common culture, beliefs and experiences. In addition, one could see society as a system of mutual benefits and burdens. It seems unfair to provide people with benefits when they do not need to deal with the burdens. Remember that Jane the American citizen may not care about anyone but herself, and her family. Because she wants safety for them, she must allow the creation of the public good for those in her own society. It would be wrong to say she values human life in general. One only needs to value one's own life to see why safety is important.

The answers to these questions depend on other factors that are not considered when justifying providing safety for those within a country. First, the third world country may not value safety or intrinsic human worth the way modern Western liberals do. Another consideration is whether it would be safe for us to help them. Lastly, it is not clear that it is right, or part of the purpose of our government, to help other nations.

Safety is extremely important and society must provide it regardless of responsibility. If we are committed to the idea that saving someone in a fire, regardless of fault, is a good thing, then we are committed to the idea of helping those who lack subsistence regardless of fault. The government is the proper entity to provide safety for two reasons. First, it is the only entity that can. Second, it is part of the government's purpose to keep people safe.*

Note:

*Special thanks to Steve Scalet, Owen Pell, John Arthur, Tony Preus, Jonathan Turbin, Gregory Sutton, Thomas Wynn, Megan Rudnick, and Edric Pauk.

Works Cited

Alexander, L. and M. Schwarzschild. (1987). 'Liberalism, Neutrality, and Equality of Welfare vs. Equality of Resources'. *Philosophy and Public Affairs*. Volume 16, 85-110.

Anderson, E. S. (1999). 'What is the Point of Equality?' *Ethics*. Volume 109, 287-337.

Arneson, R. J. (2000). 'Welfare Should Be the Currency of Justice'. *Canadian Journal of Philosophy*. Volume 30, 497-524.

Berlin, I. (1978). 'Equality'. *Concepts and Categories*. Henry Hardy (ed.). New Jersey: Princeton University Press.

Berlin, I. (1969). Four *Essays on Liberty*. Oxford: Oxford University Press.

Buchanan, A. (1985). *Ethics, Efficiency and the Market*. Maryland: Rowman and Littlefield Publishers Inc.

Cohen, G.A. (1989). 'On the Currency of Egalitarian Justice'. *Ethics*. Volume 99, 906-944.

Cupit, G. (2000). 'The Basis of Equality'. *Philosophy*. Volume 75, 105-125.

Dworkin, R. (1981). 'What is Equality? Part 2: Equality of Resources'. *Philosophy and Public Affairs*. Volume 10, 283-345.

Dworkin, R. (1986). *Law's Empire*. Massachusetts: The Belknap Press of Harvard University Press: 167-175.

Goodin, R. E. (1987). 'Egalitarianism, Fetishistic and Otherwise'. *Ethics*. Volume 98, 44-49.

Galston, W. A. (2002). 'Liberal Egalitarianism: A Family of Theories, Not a Single View." In R. C. Post and N. L. Rosenblum (eds.) *Civil Society and Government*. New Jersey: Princeton University Press, 111-122.

Kant, Immanuel. (1993). Grounding *for the Metaphysics of Morals: On a Supposed right to Lie because of Philanthropic Concerns*. 3rd ed. Trans. James W. Ellington. Indianapolis: Hackett Publishing Company, Inc.

Kolm, S. (1976). 'Public Safety'. *The American Economic Review*. Volume 66, 382-387.

Kymicka, Will. (2002). 'Civil Society and Government: A Liberal Egalitarian Perspective'. In R. C. Post and N. L. Rosenblum (eds.)

Civil Society and Government. New Jersey: Princeton University Press, 79-110.

Maynez, E. G. (1949). 'Justice and Legal Security'. *Philosophy and Phenomenological Research*. Volume 9, 496-503.

Nagel, T. (1991). *Equality and Partiality*. Oxford: Oxford University Press.

Norman, R. (1999). 'Equality, Priority, and Social Justice'. *Ratio: Journal of Analytic Philosophy*. Volume 12, 178-194.

Oi, W. Y. (1995). 'Safety at What Price?' *The American Economic Review*. Volume 85, 67-71.

Rae, D. (1981). 'Two Contradictory Ideas of (Political) Equality'. *Ethics*. Volume 91, 451-456.

Rawls, J. (1999). *A Theory of Justice*. Revised ed. Massachusetts: The Belknap Press of Harvard University Press.

Roemer, J. E. (1993). 'A Pragmatic Theory of Responsibility for the Egalitarian Planner'. *Philosophy and Public Affairs*. Volume 22, 146-166.

Runciman, W.G. (1967). 'Social' Equality'. *Philosophical Quarterly*. Volume 17, 221-230.

Sen, Amartya. (1996). 'On the Status of Equality'. *Political Theory*. Volume 24, 394-400.

Scanlon Jr., T.M. (1986). 'Equality of Resources and Equality of Welfare: A Forced Marriage'. *Ethics*. Volume 97, 111-118.

Swift, R.F. (1924). 'Security in Modern Life." *International Journal of Ethics*. Volume 34, 357-363.

Vallentyne, P. (2000). 'Equality, Efficiency, and the Priority of the Worse-Off'. *Economics and Philosophy*. Volume 16, 1-19.

Van Parijs, P. (1991). 'Why Surfers Should Be Fed: The Liberal Case for an Unconditional Basic Income'. *Philosophy and Public Affairs*. Volume 17, 101-131.

Van Parijs, P. (1995). *Real Freedom for All: What if anything can justify capitalism?* Oxford: Clarendon Press, Chapter 1.

Williams, E. B (ed.). (1991). *The Scribner-Bantam English Dictionary*. New York: Bantam Books.

Young, R. (1992). 'Egalitarianism and Personal Desert'. *Ethics*. Volume 102, 319-341.

Abstract

How should we morally assess inheritance as a social practice? In this paper I argue that instead of framing the debate within one particular tradition in political philosophy, which I call the "universalist" approach, we should look at the practice from what I call an interpretive pluralist perspective. I argue that the universalist approach is based on a flawed understanding of how we engage in moral debate and cannot be flexibly applied to the different social goals that a liberal democracy may legitimately pursue. Using the interpretive pluralist framework, I propose a way in which we may assign moral weight to principles that emanate from five different traditions in political philosophy. I connect this "weight" with background social conditions that, I argue, should play a role in how we morally assess the social practice of inheritance.

INHERITANCE AND DISTRIBUTIVE JUSTICE

AN INTERPRETIVE PLURALIST ACCOUNT

GREGORY W. SUTTON

Introduction

People begin their lives in our society from different starting points. Some people are born into extreme wealth, others are born into extreme poverty, while still others are born into situations that fit somewhere in the middle of these two extremes. It is uncontroversial that these starting points are due at least partly to the common practice of inheritance. This poses an interesting philosophical question for a liberal society, which I will explore in this paper. The question is whether or not inheritance as a social practice is morally justified. On one hand, some people view this practice as morally uncontroversial, that keeping wealth within families is a natural extension of the liberty to do what one wants with ones resources. On the other hand, this common practice has produced results that some say fundamentally violate the ideals of equality and equal opportunity for which a liberal society is supposed to stand.

What I will do in the first part of this paper is present what I think are five strong philosophical arguments regarding the morality of inheritance from different traditions in political philosophy. I will argue that each argument raises important moral principles that we should include in our moral assessment of inheritance, and that the assessment should not be framed within only one tradition in political philosophy.

This discussion will lead into my argument that a proper moral assessment of inheritance must be interpretive and pluralist. By interpretive, I mean that my theory will start with the principles raised by the arguments in Part I (but not only these principles) because they exist and are sound. That these principles exist simply means that people support them. That they are sound means that they are defensible (something I establish in Part 1). By pluralist, I mean that my theory will include all of these principles and come up with a way to weigh them in different social conditions.[1] I connect the moral weight that I assign to competing principles to these background social conditions. The key thought here is that social conditions should play a role in how we assess inheritance as a social practice; a philosophical assessment of a particular practice ought to keep in mind the practical results of its application.

Throughout the paper I defend my approach against objections that are based on a universal approach. In the last part of the paper I consider two alternative accounts of inheritance - David Haslett's argument that inheritance should be prohibited and Ed McCafferey's argument that estate taxes should be abolished.

PART I
FIVE ARGUMENTS REGARDING INHERTITANCE

An Argument Based on Natural Rights

One argument that can be made regarding the morality of inheritance can be derived from Robert Nozick's well-known book *Anarchy, State, and Utopia*. (Nozick 1974) Nozick attempts to give an alternative natural rights defense of private property, grounding his theory not in "labor-mixing" but in "entitlements." A person is entitled to his property if one of two conditions exist: the acquisition of the property was just, or, if the property was not originally acquired, the transfer of the property was just.

According to Nozick, transfers are just if they result from a free agreement among agents in conditions that are favorable to both parties. (Nozick 1974:150-182) Nozick's argument can be extended to the problem of inheritance. The argument is that inheritance should be left unregulated because it is a practice that involves entitlements that are justly transferred. There is nothing unjust, in principle, about a person giving ones property to someone else. Thus, inheritance can be regarded said as a type of just transfer.

When applied to inheritance, Nozick's rights-based theory raises important principles, the most important being liberty. Liberal democratic societies rightly take individual liberties seriously, and inheritance involves an exercise of liberty regarding property. The liberty principle will play an important role in my proposed assessment of inheritance.

An Argument Based on Desert

Moral desert raises important principles regarding inheritance. The essential principle that desert theory raises is that desert involves respect for autonomous human action which valuable in itself. (Sher 1987: 3-20) Desert theory can be extended to inheritance in the following way:

1. Autonomous choice is valuable and should be respected.
2. The decision to labor is an autonomous choice.
3. The decision to labor should be respected.
4. To respect the decision to labor means that the laborer ought to be granted ownership of the products of labor.
5. Ownership involves the ability to do what one wants with ones property, as long as such actions do not interfere with the rights of others.
6. Inheritance does not interfere with the rights of others.
7. Therefore, the practice of inheritance is morally justified.

This is by no means the only moral desert defense of inheritance that can be constructed. Indeed, it is a common claim that people who do inherit wealth did nothing to deserve it. But this claim is not as strong the argument we have constructed for two reasons. One, there does not seem to be anything morally wrong with receiving a gift. If it were wrong to receive gifts, much of our personal lives would drastically change.[2] This seems wrong because the mere fact that one does not deserve an inheritance is not grounds to tax or prohibit it; there must be other important public policy concerns. If the inheritance represents all the property the person has, we might justifiably call them lazy but cannot tax or confiscate it on desert grounds alone.

This being the case, the desert argument that defends the practice of inheritance is the stronger argument. This argument raises desert principles that we should consider in our assessment of inheritance.

An Argument Based on Equality

There are many versions of egalitarianism as a theory of political morality. Therefore, there exists a multitude of egalitarian treatments of the problem we are addressing. I will state one egalitarian argument regarding inheritance that is based on the idea that people possess equal moral worth, and that the state must respect this by showing all citizens equal concern.[3] (Dworkin 2000: 5-40) Such an argument could be constructed as follows:

1. People possess equal moral worth.
2. A just society respects this by treating people with equal concern.
3. Treating people with equal concern requires that economic inequalities be corrected by the state (where corrected means a more equal distribution).
4. Therefore, if inheritances can be demonstrated to be a source of economic inequality, then they should be taxed or prohibited.

The most important principle that this line of argument raises is that a just society must show concern for the principle of equality. This principle will also play a role in the interpretive pluralist assessment of inheritance that I defend.

An Argument Based on Social Contract

I focus now on John Rawls' social contract theory to illustrate another possible assessment of inheritance. Rawls argues that by constructing a hypothetical "original position" in which people are ignorant of race, class, and conception of the good by a "veil of ignorance" we can determine what kinds of institutions people would design, assuming that all people are indifferent to each other. (Rawls 1971: 20-55) Rawls argues that these people would choose two principles to govern these social institutions:

1. People would agree to extend basic political liberties equally and to all citizens.
2. Economic inequalities would only exist if such inequalities benefit the least advantaged members of society.

Principle one takes priority over principles two (the "difference" principle), which means that society cannot sacrifice political liberties for economic benefits. (Rawls 1971: 45-64)

How might Rawls' theory be extended to inheritance? Rawls addresses this in *A Theory of Justice*, in which he argues that an estate tax is necessary to prevent accumulations of wealth that are detrimental to liberal democracy and equal opportunity. (Rawls 1971: 277-78) This judgment is consistent with Rawls' larger political theory insofar as it flows from the principle that economic inequalities are not justified if they do not benefit the least advantaged. If the practice of inheritance contributes to inequalities that do not benefit the least advantaged, then taxation or prohibition is justified under Rawls' account.

Rawls' theory raises important principles for us to consider. One is that organized society is a cooperative venture for mutual advantage. This being the case, the state acts as a sort of mediator of conflicting interests, guided by principles Rawls thinks are compatible with what people would choose in a fair, pre-social condition. We shall see how these principles will operate in an interpretive, pluralist account of inheritance. But first let us consider one more argument based on utilitarianism.

An Argument Based on Utilitarianism

Utilitarianism as a broad moral and political theory asserts that the goal of society should be to maximize overall utility, and that public policy should be evaluated to the extent that it promotes this goal. A basic utilitarian argument regarding inheritance could be that the practice promotes overall utility. The reasons for this conclusion can widely vary.

One major argument is that private property systems maximize overall utility. One way that private systems do this is that they allow individuals to determine what they do with and how they use property; it is individuals rather than the state are best situated to make these determinations. Given that people are best situated to make decisions regarding property, a utilitarian may argue that the practice of inheritance should not be taxed for purposes of redistribution because individuals and not government know best how to distribute and make us of their resources. (Munzer 1990: 191-226)

Another reason that a utilitarian might give for not taxing or prohibiting inheritance is that the practice creates incentives for people to act in economically beneficial ways. Industriousness, technological innovation, and efficient management are all encouraged by a system that allows people both to own what they earn and transfer it as they wish. (Munzer 1990: 191-226)

Moral virtues, like industriousness and personal responsibility, are fostered in a system where people are allowed to own and transfer therefore their property. This gives the utilitarian another reason for the conclusion that inheritance supports social utility and therefore should be allowed and encouraged. (Munzer 1990:121-147)

Still other reasons based on utilitarianism lead to this conclusion. The "tragedy of the commons" example illustrates how without incentives created by private systems, people will use the land inefficiently and waste it. (Hardin 1968: 7-18) Harold Demsetz writes that Native American tribes began to create what resembled private property systems when externalities became significant and property needed to be used efficiently. (Demsetz 1983: 50-59) David Schmidtz writes that original appropriation is required if society wants to preserve its resources. (Schmidtz 1989: 8-18) It might be argued that the practice of inheritance is a legitimate way to further the interest of preservation and efficient use of scarce economic resources.

The utilitarian argument raises important considerations that my interpretive pluralist assessment of inheritance will include. The basic principle that the utilitarian argument raises is that social utility is relevant to the moral assessment of a given social practice. My interpretive theory will seek to formulate a method by which this principle may be weighed against other principles we have discussed so far.

Now that I have stated five arguments from different traditions in political philosophy, the task for an interpretive pluralist assessment is to come up with a rational way to assign weight to these principles in situations where they conflict. Before we address this issue, I must first defend my use of an interpretive pluralist approach.

PART II
INTERPRETIVE PLURALISM AND THE PRACTICE OF INHERITANCE

Definition and Justification

Interpretive political theories start with moral principles and convictions that exist and are presumptively sound. It then seeks to justify these principles. If our convictions cannot be justified, this gives us grounds to change them. John Rawls calls this "reflective equilibrium." (Rawls 1971) The preceding discussion has provided us grounds for concluding that the five arguments are sufficiently justified in a way that allows us to start our moral assessment of inheritance with them. Pluralist theories integrate different principles in ways that are theoretically sound and practically applicable. There are a variety of reasons why interpretive pluralist theories are more valuable than universal approaches. I state now a few of them.

Liberal democratic societies are characterized by the existence of competing views about public issues. Debate rages about issues like taxation, abortion rights, gun control, and freedom of speech, to name but a few. One reason why the universal approach to addressing these problems is flawed is because it ignores the moral diversity that exists in contemporary liberal democracies. The thought that only one moral value from one particular tradition in political philosophy is the only one that matters is fundamentally inconsistent with the idea of a free and open political society. Free societies allow people to choose which moral values they think ought to guide public policy. Indeed, this is an idea that justifies freedom of speech, freedom of religion, freedom of the press, and open, democratic electoral processes.

Another reason why interpretive pluralism is a sounder approach than universalism is because we do not apply the same moral principles to different political and moral questions. The debate over issues like abortion and euthanasia generally is not only about social utility, though some may indeed make arguments on these grounds. Nor are these debates only about desert or egalitarianism, though some may make arguments on these grounds as well. The point is that one universal political theory will not adequately address the diversity of political and moral controversies that arise in modern liberal democratic societies.

Most importantly, there are practical reasons why we should not suppose that only one philosophical principle ought to guide public policy. Take, for example, the debate about welfare. Some may argue on natural rights grounds that redistribution violates people's natural right to not be interfered with by the government unless they are harming someone else. Others may argue, on egalitarian grounds, that economic inequalities are unfair and should be dealt with by the state by way of taxation and redistribution. A universal political theory would seek a "winner" in this debate – which theory is theoretically "soundest." However, the results of this approach would strike us as wrong if certain social background conditions exist. If, on one hand, there exists extensive human suffering such that a significant amount of people cannot meet their basic needs and thereby not develop their human capacities, a natural rights defense against redistribution would not make sense from a practical perspective – we should not allow people to starve because of one particular conception of natural rights. If, on the other hand, most people are able to meet their basic needs, and their life prospects can reasonably be said to be within people's direct control, the egalitarian argument would lose its practical appeal if it could be shown that an estate tax would hinder economic growth in exchange for no correlative social benefit.

A related advantage of an interpretive pluralist approach is that it allows the state to legitimately pursue different goals at different times. If economic inequality is so vast that the social hopes of a significant number of people diminishes, the state may, in light of the relevant sociological data, reasonably enact a tax scheme that reduces economic inequality and thereby alleviates suffering. If, however, the same tax scheme can be shown to stifle economic growth at a time when economic inequality is not a pressing issue, and that there are more efficient schemes available, we may justifiably change the scheme. In short, political theory ought to be flexible in light of the different reasonable goals that a state may pursue in different social conditions.

There is an implied I assumption in this argument that I will now state. There is a locus of core interests that any theory of political morality worth having ought to respect. One of these core interests is that human suffering should be alleviated whenever it is reasonably possible to do so. There surely are other core interests. I will, however, only cite this one for the purposes of this paper. A political theory that binds our hands in the face of our moral obligation to alleviate human suffering when it is in our power to do so is not worthy of our support.

So we have now stated a number of reasons why interpretive pluralism is a better approach to making moral assessments about public policy issues than universalism. Now I will show how interpretive pluralism can be applied to the question of inheritance, and how one might rationally assign weight to the principles we have raised.

Applying Interpretive Pluralism to Inheritance

I propose to connect the moral weight we assign to the principles we discussed to background social conditions. By background social conditions, I mean various sociological data and information regarding people's general well being. A few examples would be data regarding gross domestic product (GDP), poverty levels, income inequalities, educational opportunity, and unemployment levels. Let us see how we can connect our moral weight assignment to one social condition – poverty levels – while we hold all other conditions constant for sake of argument.

Nozick's natural rights argument raises the principle that people have certain rights, the exercise of which must not be interfered with by other individuals or government. Within these rights is the right to not have property interests interfered with if the property is either justly acquired or justly transferred. The justification of the practice of inheritance follows from Nozick's argument insofar as it is an exercise of a property interest protected by natural rights. How should we assign weight to this principle? If there exists a significant amount of human suffering caused by poverty, and taxing inheritances can be demonstrated to be a reasonable way to alleviate this suffering, then the natural rights argument has less weight.[4] The test of reasonableness in this case comes down to a cost-benefit analysis. If the benefits of the tax on inheritance – in particular, the alleviation of human suffering – can be shown to outweigh the cost (the loss to those who make bequests and the loss to those who stand to inherit them), then sacrificing the liberty principle – that is, assigning less moral weight to it – is reasonable from a policy perspective. The core interest we have in alleviating suffering when it is reasonable to do so should not be subordinated only to a theoretical conception of the liberty principle.

Egalitarian principles should, in this case, be assigned more moral weight. The egalitarian argument I have stated is fairly clear on this – that the practice of inheritance, insofar as it causes economic inequality, should be taxed. If there exists vast economic inequalities such that some people are not capable of meeting their basic needs, then we should give more weight to this argument and less to the natural rights argument, because of the core interest we have stated. From a practical point of view, it is sensible to do this because alleviating suffering is more important than theoretical "consistency." We can allow different values to coexist without giving up any meaningful understanding of theoretical consistency.

Rawls' difference principle will also be assigned more weight in this particular situation because it furthers our core interests. Crushing poverty obviously does not benefit the least advantaged, so the difference principle would allow for an estate tax in this situation. For the same reason, however, we should assign less moral weight to the principles raised by the desert and utilitarian arguments, which, as stated, are hostile to the estate taxes. In short, the weight we assign to moral principles in situations where they compete should be guided by the extent to which they promote our core interests, one of which is alleviating extensive suffering when it is within reasonable means to do so.

There are two objections that can be raised at this point. One is that the way I have assigned weight seems to assume, without justification, a liberal egalitarian background framework insofar as it supposes that poverty is something that the state should attempt to correct. Such an objection fundamentally misunderstands the nature of the assessment I have argued for. Indeed, the interpretive pluralist assessment does the opposite – it denies that any one particular value or social goal should always guide public policy. The key claim is that the debate about the political morality of inheritance should not be couched within on particular philosophical tradition but rather within a pluralist framework that is inclusive of a variety of moral principles. The question of the morality of inheritance from an interpretive pluralist framework turns not on a particular theoretical conception of the state but rather on the reasonableness of particular public policies at different points in time. The direction of public policy would certainly change if different social conditions exist.

For example, if there exists in society relatively little poverty, where people for the most part are able to meet their basic needs, and a particular estate tax can be shown to stifle economic growth, then it is not reasonable for us to enact it because the costs of the tax outweigh the benefits. In this situation we might reasonably assign more moral weight to the principles raised by the natural rights, moral desert, and utilitarian arguments and less to the principles raised by the egalitarian and social contract arguments.

Does my approach simply endorse the status quo – does it blindly accept people's moral convictions without regard to the content of these convictions? What about moral convictions that are definitively suspect – like convictions about racial inferiority, to take one example. Interpretive pluralist theory seeks to include only those principles and social goals that are morally defensible. Indeed, part of a full account of interpretive pluralism would have to determine which principles to include and which to exclude.[5] This is beyond the scope of this paper, which only states five arguments that are defensible and illustrates how they can be weighed in an interpretive pluralist theory.

To illustrate how an interpretive pluralist assessment has worked, I now briefly allude to a historical example – the Great Depression. This example illuminates the practical advantages that my approach has over a universal approach.

The Great Depression

After the Civil War, industrialization fundamentally altered the American economy. Big corporations emerged and production underwent unprecedented increases. Americans were committed to the idea of a *laissez-faire* approach to political economy. This allowed corporations to gain more and more economic and political power. Industrialization, however, had unforeseen consequences. Working conditions deteriorated and fluctuations in the economy left people totally insecure. This culminated in the Great Depression, in which unemployment soared. Clashes between labor unions and corporations were frequent. The *laissez-faire* approach to political economy was not able to deal with these changes.

Americans compromised their commitments to *laissez-faire* capitalism so that other legitimate social goals could be pursued. The values of "rugged individualism" were assigned less moral weight than the values of other principles because of the interest in alleviating the suffering caused by the Great Depression. It was reasonable for the government to intervene in the economy in order to make life in America better. It became clear that making a public commitment to only the extreme principles of *laissez-faire* capitalism was not sensible, that only by altering these commitments to make room for other social commitments could a more workable economic system emerge. (Leuchtenburg 1963: 150-255)

How is this relevant to our discussion? Because the moral weight we assign to political principles reasonably changes in light of pressing practical considerations. If remaining theoretically "consistent" does not allow us to pursue other legitimate social goals, than theoretical consistency is not worth having, at least from a practical point of view.

Guidelines for Application

For the sake of argument, we have thus far only discussed extreme social conditions and how they might affect the weight we assign to different moral principles. There will undoubtedly be situations that do not fit these descriptions. In these situations, though the moral weight calculation will surely be more difficult to determine, the same idea applies – that moral weight should be tied to empirical social conditions so that the most practical public policies can be enacted.

There are two general conditions that can give us guidance as to when the practice the practice of tax-free inheritance become less defensible:

1. When a significant amount of people cannot meet their basic needs.
2. When inheritance can be shown to be a significant causal factor for social condition (1).
3. When it can be shown that the benefits of an estate tax scheme outweigh the costs.

If these conditions hold, then it follows that state taxation of inheritances is legitimate. The liberty, desert, and utilitarian principles are outweighed by the egalitarian and difference principles because helping people meet their basic needs is a more pressing social interest than protecting the abstract "right" to transfer property (natural rights), the need to respect autonomous action (desert), and the interest in promoting economic growth (utilitarianism).

Some Alternative Accounts

I now focus on two alternative accounts of the morality of inheritance. In an important article, David Haslett argues that gratuitous transfers should be prohibited altogether because they are contrary to the moral convictions we hold about freedom, equality, and capitalism. Conversely, Ed McCaffrey argues that estate taxes should be repealed altogether because they do not encourage beneficial individual behavior in the economic sphere. Both articles are implicitly pluralistic in nature, but they are not adequate accounts of the practice generally because they do not cover the diversity of moral principles that can reasonably be applied to the problem.

David Haslett argues that the practice of inheritance should be abolished because it is inconsistent with our convictions about free markets, equality, and equal opportunity. We do not tolerate arbitrary inequalities in political power, argues Haslett, so we should not tolerate arbitrary inequalities in economic power. The "old practice" of inheritances, therefore, should be abandoned if we want to be philosophically consistent. (Haslett 1986: 45)

It is interesting to note that Haslett's theory is based on his observations of people's convictions only about free markets, equality, and equal opportunity. What about people's convictions about natural rights and moral desert? If people only cared about free markets, capitalism, equality, and equal opportunity, Haslett's argument would be strong. However, because we also value economic growth, and because there could exist situations in which an estate tax would significantly hinder economic growth, Haslet's account in incomplete. Because of this, Haslett's contention that we should abolish altogether the practice of inheritance lacks sufficient justification.

Ed McCaffrey argues that, given the overwhelming public support of Americans to lower or eliminate estate taxes, an interpretive theory yields the conclusion that we should eliminate the estate tax altogether. He argues that estate taxes do not raise nearly enough revenue to correct inequalities in wealth and income, and that they do not encourage socially beneficial individual economic behavior, like savings. According to McCaffrey, estate taxes provide no incentive for anybody, rich or not rich, to engage in savings because such savings will be heavily taxed. Rather, an estate tax encourages consumption during ones lifetime to avoid this tax. McCaffrey further argues that we are not opposed to individuals holding a lot of wealth. What we are opposed to is certain ways in which people use this wealth, such as exercising undue influence in the political system or over-consumption, which has adverse effects on the whole economy. McCaffrey concludes that a progressive consumption tax would be better than a progressive estate tax. (McCaffrey 1994: 57-68)

McCaffrey's interpretive account is important because it illustrates the complexity of the question at hand and the importance of taking into account actual social data when making moral assessments. McCaffrey's article can be read as saying that estate taxes are not justified when they are not, in fact, achieving their purported social goals, namely correcting inequalities in wealth. As I argued earlier, however, this strongly depends on the social details. It could be the case that estate taxes do, if not correct, *prevent* accumulations in wealth that are detrimental to a liberal society. It could also be the case that estate taxes do *help* alleviate, though not *totally* alleviate, human suffering caused by crushing poverty. While it may be true that such taxes encourage consumption, the overall goal of the tax could be to prevent wealthy people from exercising undue influence on the political system. The goal might also be to alleviate poverty; encouraging economically beneficial behavior would be ancillary to this goal. While it may be the case that estate taxes are not achieving their purported ends, this is not always the case. Extensive sociological research would be needed to make this assessment. If McCaffrey's observations do in fact hold, then his proposed consumption tax may be a necessary and even better alternative to the estate tax. An interpretive pluralist theory would allow for this because it is tied closely with the practical results of application. McCaffrey's work simply raises another option that can be looked from an interpretive pluralist perspective.

Conclusion

I hope by now that it is evident that interpretive pluralism is a sound approach to the question of the morality of inheritance. I will now briefly summarize what I have said.

I first stated five arguments from five different traditions in political philosophy. I argued that each argument raises principles that are important for an adequate assessment of the morality of inheritance, and that the mere reason that they are from different philosophical traditions should not lead us to either give up the assessment or try and find one overarching principle. This led me to my defense of an interpretive pluralist, rather than a universal, approach to the practice of inheritance. I argued that the interpretive pluralist approach is better than the universal approach because it takes into account the reality of different social conditions, the existence of which affects the defensibility of a given political theory. I then proposed a set of guidelines that would affect the weight assigned to different principles in situations where they compete. Finally, I considered two alternative accounts of the practice of inheritance and argued that both are based on incomplete pictures of the diversity of moral principles that that should be included in a complete moral assessment of the practice.

Defending interpretive pluralism as a sound general approach for political philosophy could not be done within the limits of a single paper. However, beyond providing arguments about how pluralism works for assessing the practice of inheritance, I suggest that this approach might open up new ways of thinking about other problems in political philosophy. Political theory should be able to practically account for the reality of pressing social problems like poverty, racism, crime, and economic inequality in addition to formulating sound, abstract philosophical doctrine. While the latter pursuit is certainly a valuable enterprise, serious inquiry about the central questions of social institutions must also bear in mind the practical results of applying political theories if we are to regard such inquiry as worthy of serious pursuit.

Notes:

1 It should be noted that the theory presented here is not meant to be exhaustive. Indeed, there may be other principles that can be included in a pluralist account of inheritance. The five arguments are only meant to show why a pluralist approach is a good approach to assessing the practice.

2 We would have to abolish the whole practice of gift-giving on grounds that receivers of gifts do not deserve them.

3 It should be noted, however, that even egalitarian arguments that

share this fundamental principle will vary in form and will arrive at somewhat different conclusions.

4 I define poverty as a condition in which a person cannot meet his or her basic needs, like food, clothing, and shelter. The list of basic needs can be more expansive, but I leave this question open to further argument.

5 This would probably be the subject of a book.

6 I would like to thank Professor Steven Scalet for making this honors project a possibility, Professor John Arthur for his invaluable advice and instruction, and Owen Pell for his generous support for the honors program. I would also like to thank Adam Ross, Jonathan Turbin, and Thomas Wynn for their helpful commentary on this paper. I would finally like to thank Levia Airall for her unending support.

Reference

Berlin, Isaiah. *Four Essays on Liberty*. Oxford: Oxford University Press, 1969.

Christman, John. *The Myth of Property*. Oxford: Oxford University Press, 1990.

Demsetz, Harold. "Toward a Theory of Property Rights", *The American Economic Review*, Vol. 57, No. 2, Papers and Proceedings of the Seventy-ninth Annual Meeting of the American Economic Association. (May, 1967), pp. 347-359.

Dworkin, Ronald. *Law's Empire*. Cambridge: Harvard University Press, 1986.

Dworkin, Ronald. *Sovereign Virtue: The Theory and Practice of Equality*. Cambridge: Harvard University Press, 2000.

Dworkin, Ronald. "What is Equality? Part 1: Equality of Welfare", *Philosophy and Public Affairs*, Vol. 10, No. 3. (Summer, 1981), pp. 185-246.

Dworkin, Ronald. "What is Equality? Part 2: Equality of Resources", *Philosophy and Public Affairs*, Vol. 10, No. 4. (Autumn, 1981), pp. 283-345.

Dworkin, Ronald. "Objectivity and Truth: You'd Better Believe It." *Philosophy and Public Affairs*, Vol. 25, No. 2. (Spring, 1996), pp. 87-139.

Hardin, Garrett. "The Tragedy of the Commons", *Science*. 1968, 168, 1,243-8.

Haslett, David. "Is Inheritance Justified?", *Philosophy and Public Affairs*, Vol. 15, No. 2. (Spring, 1986), pp. 122-155.

Leuchtenburg, William. *Franklin D. Roosevelt and the New Deal*. New York: Harpur and Row, 1963.

McCafferey, Edward. "The Political Liberal Case Against the Estate Tax", *Philosophy and Public Affairs*, Vol. 23, No. 4. (Autumn, 1994), pp. 281-312.

Mill, John Stuart. *Utilitarianism*. Indianapolis: Bobbs-Merril, 1957. (Originally published 1861)

Munzer, Stephen. *A Theory of Property*. Cambridge: Cambridge University Press, 1990.

Nozick, Robert. *Anarchy, State, and Utopia*. New York: Basic Books, 1974.

Rawls, John. *A Theory of Justice*. Cambridge: Harvard University Press, 1971.

Rawls, John. *Political Liberalism*. New York: Columbia University Press, 1993.

Rawls, John. *Justice as Fairness: A Restatement*. Cambridge: Harvard University Press 2001.

Schmidtz, David. "When Is Original Appropriation Required?", *Monist*, 1990, pg. 504-519.

Sher, George. *Desert*. Princeton: Princeton University Press, 1987.

Walzer, Michael, *Spheres of Justice: A Defense of Pluralism and Equality*. New York: Basic Books, 1983.

Abstract

The ability to achieve deliberative democracy rests, as Jurgen Habermas asserts, upon a transition in the structural *form* of political dialogue. Habermas' claim that the implementation of just procedures is at the heart of this transition, is correct. However, for just political discussions to occur, one must be able to foster relationships in which the procedures of communicative ethics can be practiced effectively. Procedures can *instruct* one to talk and listen, but dialogue has to be invited by the participants themselves. To achieve the goals of Habermas' politically legitimate procedures, one must, therefore, understand what it means to change the human condition such that people can enter into relationships that promote polyphonic dialogue. Focusing, as Martin Buber does, on the dialogical aspect of human relationships, offers an instructive view of what it means to engage in the type of polyphonic dialogues that deliberative democratic theorists strive to achieve.

DELIBERATIVE DIALOGUE AND THE NEED FOR FOSTERING DIALOGICAL RELATIONSHIPS

Anna Feigenbaum*

Students recently participated in a rally on my university's campus to promote awareness about the Israeli/Palestinian conflict. Students in one group protested Arafat's terrorism and the suicide bombings occurring in Israel. They chanted things such as, "Anti-Zionism is anti-Semitism," waved pickets and wrapped themselves in Israel flags. Standing a few yards away were the People for Palestinians who countered with arguments that Palestinian refuges be allowed to return to their homeland. While walking by the protest, a classmate turned to me and said, "This is so stupid. They are both screaming for peace."

Polarized arguments like this one result from overemphasis on disagreement. Although this rally was meant to raise awareness, all it did raise was the noise level. Unfortunately, this type of communication occurs on a regular basis. Deliberative democratic theories propose various solutions to address the failure of political dialogues such as the one above. These theories center around the question of what constitutes admissible content in political dialogue and how this content should be presented and received. I wish to propose that in addition to creating procedures for political discussions, people must foster dialogical relationships in order to solve the problems of polarization and engage in *real* dialogue.

Objecting to the John Rawls' original position and theory of what constitutes acceptable public reasons, Jurgen Habermas argues that focus should be placed on the form rather than the content of dialogue. In order to understand the reason for this change, I will discuss some of the objections Habermas, as well as Michael Sandel make to John Rawls' theory of public reason. I will show that a content-oriented approach will only delay and deter engagement in deliberative dialogues. Instead, I will argue that what is needed are polyphonic or multi-voiced, collective dialogues such as those supported by Habermas' theory of communicative ethics. I will point out that focusing, as Habermas does, on the structure of dialogue will reveal the importance of fostering the dialogical relationships necessary for achieving polyphonic dialogues.

Procedures instructing one to listen, comprehend, and be fair-minded can come in many different degrees. Even when viewing the other as an opponent in a polarized dialogue, it is still possible to reflect on what the other says. The kind of virtues needed for *real* dialogue, however, call for people to view the other not as an opponent but as a *real* person with a different conception of how to achieve the common good. It is only after two *real* people encounter each other that moral insight becomes possible. Dialogical relationships must be fostered in order for participants to engage in an honest discourse that moves beyond conventional morality.

Addressing the problems of *polarization* that occur as a result of failed dialogues, as seen at the peace rally, I will discuss how the philosophy of Martin Buber can help one re-conceive of his or her relationships with others in the way necessary for Habermas' communicative ethics to be practiced effectively.

Debate over appropriate substantive content arises from different conceptions of the self as embodied in the liberal theories of John Rawls, the communicative ethics theories of Jurgen Habermas and the communitarian theories such as that of Michael Sandel. On the one end of the spectrum lies the liberal self-image, on the other the idea of the encumbered self. Rawls' notion of public reason rises out of his idea of the original position. Rawls' believes that rational individuals have the ability to set aside the attributes that make them different. In the Rawlsian conception of liberal politics participants must "bracket off" their nonpublic and associational motives and beliefs, and enter a public political sphere with only their reasonable public reasons. According to Rawls, public reason is public in three ways: (1) it is the reason of the public; (2) its nature and content is public and it is conducted open to public view; (3) its subject is the good of the public and matters of fundamental justice (Rawls 1997: 93).

Communitarians like Michael Sandel object to this Rawlsian 'liberal self-image' that is presupposed by the Rawlsian understanding of the very possibility of public reason. In *Democracy's Discontent*, Sandel writes, "Liberal justice is blind to such differences between persons as race, religion, ethnicity, and gender, for in the liberal self-image, these features do not really define our identity in the first place. They are not constituents but merely attributes of the self, the sort of things the state should look beyond" (Sandel 1996: 13) Communitarian theory suggests instead that personal reasons should not only have a place in dialogue, but because they flow from and express who we are, they must play a significant role in dialogue. Sandel believes that to "veil" aspects of the self from political discussions is to deny an integral part of the human condition.

The weakness of this objection is not in its aim, but in that it misunderstands Rawls's position. The notion that reasons in deliberative dialogue should be 'public' does not simply mean that they should avoid reference to the personal, but that their subject and their content must regard the "good of the public and matters of fundamental justice." Communitarians conjoin the idea of 'public reason' with the notion of a 'liberal self-image.' Their objection focuses on the idea that the personal cannot be detached from the public. However, Rawls's objective is not to deny identity, but rather to usurp it with reason, a reason that is aimed not to the good of the individual (or his or her association), but to the common good of the public. Matthew Festestein writes that "People who are compelled to offer arguments in terms of public reasons will over time begin to think in terms of public reasons, and will tend not to conceive of their own interests or identities as opposed to public statement" (Festenstein 1999: 158)

My objection to Rawls' "veil of ignorance" is slightly different from that of the communitarians'. Festestein clearly outlines Rawls' aim. The goal is to advance the way that people *conceive* of public interests. Under the "veil of ignorance" one does not know anything about what I shall call his or her 'my' (my race, my religion, my gender, etc.). Thus, the reasons offered would be reasons that any person could give or accept regardless of the life they had once the veil has lifted. My objection is not that it is necessarily impossible to detach oneself from one's 'my' when offering reasons, but that doing so is not helpful for achieving the polyphonic dialogues necessary for moral insight.

A Rawlsian content-oriented approach to dialogue would result in a failure to understand and incorporate differences. Rawls purports that the only important voice in a political discussion is the voice of pure, public reason. This emphasis on curbing nonpublic reasons from entering political discussions moves one away from the goal of achieving an intersubjective dialogue made up by *real* people. A *real* person and a *real* discussion do not have only one voice—that of pure public reason—rather, both are polyphonic or multi-voiced. Thus, it is not that it is impossible to reason without considering 'my' reasons, it is that one can reasonably offer 'my' reasons into a dialogue without jeopardizing it. Furthermore, offering 'my' reasons advances polyphonic dialogue by allowing more voices (or reasons) to enter the discussion. The more reasonably offered reasons, the more understanding and incorporation of differences and thus, the greater the possibility for moral insight.

As Habermas writes, "Liberal misgivings about opening up an unrestricted spectrum of public issues and topics are not justified so long, at least, as the personal integrity of the individual is preserved" (Habermas as cited in Freeman 2000: 407). Rawls theory, he contends, mistakenly assumes that an individual, rational thinker can reason (in the original position) to real conclusions about what fundamental civil and political rights should be. Habermas, like Sandel, wishes to move away from a harsh public/nonpublic divide and focus instead on the "conditions of rational discourse and negotiations" (Habermas as cited in Freeman 2000: 378). Habermas is less concerned with the *content* and more concerned with the *form* of dialogue. Habermas stresses that the importance of deliberation is the process of dialogue itself. Deliberation must occur between *real,* polyphonic people who not only have the capacity to reason but are also made up of 'my' attributes.

Content-oriented supporters of deliberative democracy, like John Rawls, see dialogue as merely a forum for different individuals to offer reasonable opinions. These opinions are 'put into the pool' for others to reflect upon. When everyone has had an opportunity to put forth his or her view, dialogue has occurred. Equality of participation or even the opportunity to participate justifies the procedure. Thus, the procedure, because it shelters the public from the private, justifies the policy via its use. Habermas challenges this notion on the grounds that it is insufficient to simply put opinions into the pool. Habermas says, "Moral justifications are dependent on argumentation actually being carried out, not for pragmatic reasons of an equalization of power, but for internal reasons, namely that real argument makes moral insight possible" (Habermas as cited in Freeman 2000: 385). For Habermas, it is the exchange of ideas and the process of dialogue itself that makes moral insight a real possibility.

Shifting focus from the content to the form of dialogue does not promise an absence of disagreements. Nor does it suggest that the desire to achieve collective good will always usurp individual moral convictions. Rather, it is an approach that presumes moral insight results from polyphonic rather than restricted dialogues. Polyphonic dialogues are thus justifiable, not only because they implement procedural ideas of equal participation, but also because moral insight is made possible by participating in them. So, while Habermas' notion of pure procedural justice holds something similar Rawls's, namely that if procedures for deliberative discussions are just, what emerges from those discussions must be just, unlike Rawls, Habermas' procedure does not restrict at the outset what can enter the procedure. This shift in focus, from the content to the form of dialogue, stresses the importance of interaction between participants in a political discussion. Although Habermas and Rawls both hold, along with other deliberative democratic theorists, that engaging in real dialogue requires certain procedures necessary for interaction, Habermas makes the stronger claim that practicing these procedures legitimizes the outcome of political dialogues. What I wish to argue is that the shift in focus from content to form calls not only for the implementation of procedures but for a reconceptualization of the relationships necessary for *real* dialogue to occur.

Procedure can *instruct* one to talk and listen, but dialogue has to be invited by the participants themselves. The ability to achieve deliberative democracy rests, as Habermas asserts, upon a transition in the structural *form* of political dialogue. Habermas' claim that the implementation of just procedures is at the heart of this transition, is correct. However, for just political discussions to occur, one must be able to foster relationships in which the procedures of communicative ethics can be practiced effectively. As Alexander Sidorkin writes, "Policies do not respond to the dialogical, which is a fundamental aspect of being human, and they are not suitable for the task of changing human conditions" (Sidorkin 1999: 36) To achieve the goals of Habermas' politically legitimate procedures, one must understand what it means to change the human condition such that people can enter into relationships that promote polyphonic dialogue.

I will begin my argument from here. Using Martin Buber's discussion of the self and the other, I will explain how one can begin to conceive of human relationships in a manner that is compatible with the ideals of deliberative democracy. Focusing, as Buber does, on the dialogical aspect of human relationships, offers an instructive view of what it means to engage in polyphonic dialogues.

As Habermas suggests, one must focus on incorporating different views and engaging in *real* argumentation to achieve polyphonic dialogues. However, the reason that dialogues fail is not only because of a lack of procedural guidelines, but also because of a failure in relation. If one looks at the ways that the failure to incorporate differences manifests itself in dialogue, one can see that solutions lay not only in procedural remedies, but in a re-conception of the way human beings behave as selves and with others.

Differences work against achieving dialogue in two ways, by *polarizing* positions in the dialogue and by *polarizing* participants in the dialogue. Polarization of positions occurs when participants aim at self-affirmation rather than at agreement, or at least, at understanding the other's position. Participants also become polarized when marginalization occurs in dialogue. Marginalization occurs when the voice of an individual or group of individuals is included in dialogue but that inclusion is manipulated by the majority of the group. For example, in conversations about homosexual rights, bisexuals are sometimes marginalized because of a bias toward their sexual orientation. Both polarizing positions and polarizing participants by marginalizing them are characteristic of failed relationships; they work against achieving the polyphonic dialogue necessary for moral insight.

Maurice Friedman writes that, "Polarization leads to *willful* misunderstanding in which people refuse to see the position of others from within...whatever they hear is fitted into either/or of those who are *for* them or those who are *against* them...the other is a caricature and you are a caricature and there is mutual mistrust" (Friedman in Arnett 1986: xiv). Humans, according to Ronald Arnett, often engage in polarized communication because it "neatly organizes events into contrasting categories, giving the illusion of sharpness of perception, when in reality there is a refusal to gain new insights by listening to others (Arnett 1986: 34)." For example, if I am avidly against the idea of legalizing marijuana and I engage in a conversation with someone who supports legalization, I may assume that they are therefore entirely opposed to my beliefs and have nothing to offer because of this difference. If the other person discusses medical benefits of marijuana use, I would dismiss them because they support legalization and oppose prohibition. In this way I have characterized myself as *for* prohibition, the other as *against* prohibition and I have fit the argument for medical use of marijuana into one of these contrasting categories. In psychology this propensity to over categorize is known as the *assimilation bias*.

We assimilate new information into schemas. "A schema is a cognitive structure that organizes our knowledge, beliefs, and past experiences, thereby providing a framework for understanding new events and future experiences" (Levy 1997: 137). Assimilation helps one process new information. In many cases assimilating new information is not only useful but also necessary. However, when assimilation is over relied on, psychologists say that one is practicing the *assimilation bias.* We practice the *assimilate bias* when:

> [We incorporate new information into our schemas] even if it means changing or distorting the information itself...Schemas bias our

> perception, processing, and interpretation in the direction of confirming our expectations...we tend to overlook, misconstrue, and even reject valid information when it is not consistent with our schemas...the assimilation bias represents a significant obstacle to clear thinking and effective problem-solving (Levy 1997: 137).

In the above example, I am assimilating the new information (an argument for medical marijuana use) into my schema (pro-legalization arguments that I do not agree with). In doing so I am not really listening to the argument for medical use, rather I am categorizing it as 'something I am opposed to.' The way to tackle problems of assimilation bias and polarized conversation is to *accommodate* rather than *assimilate* information. One accommodates when one "changes pre-existing beliefs so that they make room for new information" (Levy 1997: 137). If I were accommodating the argument for medical marijuana use, I would have to be willing to alter my schema. Instead of assuming that I disagree with the argument because it does not affirm my belief, I would have to listen to the argument and then ask myself if supporting medical use necessarily fit into either pole—legalization or prohibition—or if instead there was something other than just two sides, for and against legalization.

In *I and Thou* Martin Buber addresses the problem of assimilation, stating, "The obstacle: for the improvement of the capacity for experience and use generally involves a decrease in man's power to relate" (Buber 1970: 89). Buber writes that the process of assimilation, which he calls experience and use, is part of the I-it district. The I-it association is a relation of self to object. It is dangerous to always assimilate when we relate to others through dialogue because assimilation uses and experiences people and their opinions as if they were objects. Buber writes, "There are not two kinds of human beings, but there are two poles of humanity." In everyone there is pure person and pure ego. "The person beholds his self; the ego occupies himself with his my: my manner, my race, my looks, my genius" (Buber 1970: 114).

The ego is unable to relate because he is too overcome by himself, and thus can only see the other and his or her opinion as an object.

Listening to each other's feelings is often viewed as the answer to relational failures. As discussed earlier, Sandel believes that the liberal self-conception is so devoid of the personal (my manner, my race) that under a Rawlsian scheme, people would be unable to engage in successful political dialogue. Rejecting this type of claim, Buber writes, "Those who suffer because institutions yield no public life have thought of a remedy: feelings are to loosen up or thaw or explode the institutions, as if they could be renewed by feelings, by introducing the freedom of feelings" (Buber 1970: 93). Buber here makes light of the idea that sharing one's 'feelings' is central to fostering relationships. By 'feelings,' Buber is referring to reasons that come from the pure ego, or in other words, reasons that are *only* motivated by the 'my' (my religion, my race, etc.) Buber, like Habermas, acknowledges that admitting nonpublic reasons may be a necessary part of a discussion, however, they are not in themselves a solution to the problems of failed dialogue. As will be shown later, problems arise, not when 'my' reasons are part of the *content* of dialogue, but when they control the interactions occurring in the dialogue.

Rawls attempts to circumvent the entire issue of interacting through 'my' reasons by bracketing them from conversation. The reason that Habermas, Buber, Sandel and Sidorkin object to this approach is simply because 'my' reasons can be reasonable and they often underlie or overlap one's seemingly public opinions. Thus, their inclusion in dialogue is not negative, but rather can sometimes increase or clarify our comprehension of the other's position. For example, if Sally, a Muslim, and Ed, an atheist, are engaging in a discussion about public school prayer, restricting the inclusion of their 'my,' in this case their religion, will only delay the progress of dialogue as can be shown through a simple scenario:

> **Sally:** I believe there should be designated times and places for students to pray if they want. Everyone should have the right to choose to practice their faith.
>
> **Ed:** We are talking about public school; therefore, having time for prayer or any religious activity during the school day is inappropriate.

Ed and Sally both appear to be offering what Rawls would deem 'public reasons'. Differences in their views can be attributed to different conceptions of what rights like freedom of religion, and political arrangements like separation of church and state, entail. Sally thinks that the right to pray during the school day is implied in the notion of freedom of religion, whereas Ed sees separation of church and state to mean that the freedom of religion only allows for prayer when outside of a public institution (in this case a public school). Sally and Ed can continue this discussion of how freedom of religion should be interpreted and applied, offering public reasons for the acceptance of either view. However, what would happen if they engaged in a less restricted dialogue?

> **Sally:** In my religion we must pray five times a day. This is very hard for the children when they do not have the opportunity to take a break from their day. I do not think that all children should have to pray, but what can it hurt to give those who wish to practice their faith the opportunity to?
>
> **Ed:** But to allot time for prayer, while maybe benefiting religious students, will only ostracize non-religious students. If parents want students to pray they can send them to private schools.

Now that Sally has put her 'my' (my religion, my children) into the conversation, what has changed? Emergence of these 'my' reasons in dialogue is only detrimental to the dialogue if Sally is unable to accept Ed because of them or if Ed rejects what Sally has said in light of them. If Sally were to affirm that her 'my' reasons justified her opinion and falsified everything Ed had to say because it did not affirm her beliefs, she would be polarizing the conversation and exhibiting an assimilation bias. Ed's opinion would not be seen as something important offered into a pool of collective knowledge by another, but as an object that she could dismiss because it did not fit into her preexisting schema. Likewise, if Ed rejected Sally's opinion because of his atheism, he too would be prematurely relying on the presupposed truth of his beliefs.

Furthermore, 'my' reasons are often beneficial because they offer another voice or perspective in a polyphonic dialogue. Although 'my' reasons may not necessarily add weight to an opinion, they can be seen to add to the 'intersubjective perspective' that dialogue is able to create. Accommodating one's views to accept another's does not imply that one must give up one's own convictions, but that one 'change his or her preexisting beliefs to make room for new information.' Furthermore, Ed can still justifiably choose not to abandon his opinion in light of Sally's reasons, while still viewing her as a person and allowing her opinion to influence his own. Having listened to Sally's appeal, Ed can decide that it is not strong enough to override the importance of keeping prayer out of public schools. Either way, Sally has influenced Ed's opinion so long as Ed has accommodated his preexisting beliefs to fit her argument. For example, prior to their exchange, Ed may have believed that 'all religious families want prayer in school' or that 'all religious families supporting prayer in school are doing so for their own benefit.' Having cognitive flexibility means that Ed can change these beliefs and focus not on *for* and *against* categorizations, but rather on gaining an intersubjective perspective on the issue.

Accommodating one's beliefs to include the information offered by another's while maintaining one's position has more merit in the unrestricted scenario than in the Rawlsian or bracketed scenario. Hearing strong arguments that oppose our own can increase the flexibility of one's views whether it alters them or makes them stronger.

Cognitive flexibility refers to this ability to recast one's ideas in light of new information. This is why, as Habermas aptly points out, the particular substantive content of a moral argument is less important than the *form* of argumentation having a polyphonic structure. Only polyphonic arguments are capable of incorporating differences in nonpolarized ways such that moral insights can be reached. Turning now to the Bubarian idea of relational reciprocity, I will discuss the necessity of fostering relationships and forming *dialogical* communities in order to achieve polyphonic dialogues, thus creating the possibility for moral insight.

Buber writes that the two necessary conditions for the emergence of community are that all people "have to stand in a living, reciprocal relationship to a single living center, and they have to stand in a living reciprocal relationship to one another" (Buber 1970: 94). If we understand what these two conditions mean for Buber's notion of community, we can see that living, reciprocal relationships also lie at the heart of deliberative democracy.

The claim that persons must "stand in a living, reciprocal relationship with a single living center," is admittedly obscure, but seems to mean that persons (if taken as citizens) are members of a place (perhaps a state) and that a living (ongoing) relationship exists between the two. Personifying a state allows one to think about it as engaging in a relationship. It is necessary that one does this in order to discuss political obligations and responsibilities. Most conceptions of deliberative democracies agree that there is a relationship between state and citizen, and that that relationship can be seen as something reciprocal in which people have an interest in the affairs of their state and the state has an interest in certain affairs of its people. The second component of Buber's community is more difficult to understand.

For a living, reciprocal relationship to be fostered among people, they must, as we have just discussed, be willing to accommodate their beliefs to include new information. To do this, one must give up the idea that there is only singular ownership over meaning and one must not view language and knowledge as possessions. Similar to the problems of polarization that arise from our inability to accommodate other's moral/political views, our tendency to argue against each other's imagined rather than real positions, leads to failed relationships and thus, failed dialogues. Just as polarized moral arguments are generally self-affirming they view meaning as something individual and internal. The problem of singular ownership over meaning arises when one assumes that pure ego or pure self motivates the other's meaning. Or in other words, that meaning is entirely selfish and based on 'my' reasons, or entirely selfless and based on others' 'my' reasons. According to Arnett, one does not accept the other as a *real* person, when one is "constantly hypothesizing about the latent or unconscious meaning" in what the other says (Arnett 1986: 49-50). Hidden motives may exist, but when one constantly anticipates them, one cannot engage in *real* dialogue. Presupposing the other's claims are that of a pure ego, secretly motivated or only motivated by nonpublic interests, leads to further polarization. One regresses into combative dialogue, protecting his or her now threatened ego by attacking the other's position. At the same time, it is wrong to assume the other acts as a pure person, always offering only public justifications for his or her beliefs. This reverse attitude is just as much a hazard to dialogue because taking either of these stances makes the claim that the self has a greater knowledge of the other's motives than the other does without making a real attempt to discover what those motives are. Regardless of whether one sees the other as pure ego or pure person, he or she does not see a *real* person. Encountering people as images or caricatures "will only augment isolation from one another" and avoid the interdependency needed for *real dialogue* (Arnett 1986).

Returning to the dialogue between Sally and Ed, one can see the effects of treating a *real* person as a pure person or a pure ego. Looking again at the second exchange, in which Sally unveils her 'my', one can see how and why polarization occurs:

> **Sally:** In my religion we must pray five times a day. This is very hard for the children when they do not have the opportunity to take a break from their day. I do not think that all children should have to pray, but what can it hurt to give those who wish to practice their faith the opportunity to?

Interpreting what Sally *means* as if she were a pure ego, Ed would conclude that Sally's appeal has no merit because she is trying to put the interest of the her association (religion, family) over collective interests. Ed would claim that Sally *meant* to assert the special rights of her faction. On the other hand, if Ed viewed Sally as a pure person, he would interpret what she said as if she were a martyr, appealing solely to the struggle children face (being unable to pray) and the community's responsibility to alleviate their hardship (by allotting them time to do so). The problem with each of these meanings that Ed has ascribed to Sally's words is a result of his failure to follow procedures to be 'fair-minded' and to 'really listen.' However, underlying those problems is a deeper problem displayed in Ed's reaction. Ed assumes meaning, rather than attempting to discover it. The pure ego/pure person failure of political discussion is a result of both a failure to practice communicative ethics as well as a reluctance to foster dialogical relationships. Ed must talk to, and not at, Sally if he wants to find out what she *really means.*

Before examining misuses of language, I believe it is necessary to respond further to the Rawlsian argument that bracketing nonpublic interests from dialogue will alleviate the problems associated with 'my' reasons. The bracketing solution seems, at first, appealing. Disallowing nonpublic reasons in dialogue would certainly limit the number of times motives are misrepresented. How could one claim the other was acting as pure ego if the ego was restricted from conversation?

Allowing 'my' reasons into dialogue poses the problem of determining that those reasons have a communal rather than associational motive. A communal motive comes from a desire for the public good;

an associational motive is a 'my' motive, spawning from a desire to affirm the position or promote the special interests of 'my' association. Rawls' answer to this problem is to mandate that all reasons be communal. But why avoid a problem when solving it is both feasible and beneficial to the larger task of forming reciprocal relationships in which the 'my' doesn't degrade human integrity? Alexander Sidorkin argues, "The greatest failing of our civilization is its inability to deal with difference. Our irrational, panicky response to difference betrays our narcissistic longing for sameness...Instead one may consider difference a quality, or function of relation" (Sidorkin 1999: 30). As I will now discuss, a collective view of meaning and language can help one incorporate differences into dialogue.

The interdependency needed for *real* dialogue requires a view of language as something that is not only individual but collective. To understand the value of conceiving of language as something collective, one must give up the narrow view that language is merely a tool humans use to communicate beliefs. Martin Buber argues that, "In truth language does not reside in man but man stands in language and speaks out of it" (Buber 1970: 89). Broadening the view of language does not refute theories of meaning, but rather encourages participants to work with each other to achieve polyphonic dialogue. Theories of meaning generally fall into one of three categories: ideational, behavioral, or referential. The ideational theory of meaning claims that the words one uses represent the ideas in one's mind, whereas the behavioral theory argues that the words one chooses are for one's intended hearers. In the behavioral model, words gain meaning not in oneself, but in others. Referential theories take a different approach, claiming that meanings lie outside of both oneself and one's words, instead they refer to something external that one wishes to speak about (Hacking 1975: 1-7). The collective theory of language that I purpose is not an alternative theory of meaning. The ideational, behavioral, and referential theories look at the *meaning* of individuals, whereas I am interested in looking at how dialogical interaction can construct collective meaning, which might be understood by the collective as ideational, behavioral, or referential.

Collective meaning, as I call it here, is the constructed meaning agreed upon and understood by all participants such that everyone's individual meaning is being fairly represented by the words or the exchange of words being used. Returning to the discussion between Sally and Ed, one can understand what constructing collective meaning means. Note here that Ed's response to Sally claims her position is one that "benefits religious students."

> **Ed:** But to allot time for prayer, while maybe benefiting religious students, will only ostracize non-religious students. If parents want students to pray they can send them to private schools.

Explaining what she *means*, while appreciating the difference of Ed's position, Sally could respond:

> **Sally:** I see what you are saying. But I do not think that time for prayer benefits religious students. It is not a privilege to practice your religion.
>
> **Ed:** I did not mean to say that it was, what I mean is that public schools should not allot time for religious practice because not all students are religious. It is not a privilege to practice your religion, but it is something that special time is being allotted for. That is why I think that religion is something that should be practiced privately.
>
> **Sally:** Religion is not like a sport. You do not practice after school, take off your uniform and go home. My religion is my way of life.

Sally and Ed are not just offering opinions on an external subject (school prayer), they are engaging in a dialogue that uses language to discover what the other *means* and to give reasons for their beliefs in a way that the other can understand. Ed's suggestion that time for prayer is a 'benefit' sparked a response from Sally in part because each had a different understanding of what was meant by the word benefit. Similarly, Sally's argument that one does not simply 'practice' religion resulted from the fact that she saw the word as meaning, in this context, something different from what Ed meant by it. Both of these words are only understood after Ed and Sally have engaged in a dialogue that works toward constructing a collective meaning. Following the exchange, both Ed and Sally's opinions have been clarified, not only because they have followed procedures to listen and be fair-minded, but because they used dialogue to achieve a collective understanding of meaning. They displayed cognitive flexibility in the 'new context' of their discussion by allowing language to be flexible. Now it is possible for Sally and Ed to argue each other's *real* and not *imagined* positions.

The second task necessary for accommodating beliefs in order to foster the reciprocal relationships needed to make moral insight possible, is arriving at a view of knowledge that shows concern for the self, the other, and the relationship. There are three ways to view the exchange of knowledge. I have named them, the ego-centric view, the self-actualization view, and the relational view. I shall argue that the only way to achieve the type of dialogue necessary for *real* political discussion is to adopt the relational view of knowledge.

Concerned entirely with self-affirmation, the ego views knowledge as an object to use and acquire. This ego-centric view of knowledge results in an inability to form anything other than I-it relationships. As Martin Buber suggests, "The ego tries to possess as much as possible" (Buber 1970:114). One who claims possession over information is prone to offer evidence only in support of his or her views, never directly in promotion of the dialogue itself. Knowledge, viewed as such, functions as something one can use to 'prove one's point,' or acquire to advance one's position. The ego says either, "I will give you knowledge so that you can agree with my beliefs," or "I will listen to you so I can take knowledge from you to satisfy my beliefs."

This view of knowledge results in polarization. In aiming to strengthen one's position, the ego categorizes information into a "for and against model," isolating the self from the other. This view of exchanging knowledge cannot be part of *real* dialogue because its ultimate concern for the ego or self is inconsistent with the goal of creating reciprocal relationships.

The self-actualized view of exchanging knowledge is often mistaken for *real* dialogue. This view shows concern for self and other, in that participants practice communicative ethics. However, knowledge is only shared to strengthen each individual's beliefs. In this view, the self says, "I will listen to you to gain more knowledge" or "I will give you knowledge so that you can gain more knowledge." The self and other can, in this view, accommodate new information. However, the goal of their accommodation is not a collective goal, rather an individual one.

This view parallels the idea of putting opinions into a pool. Looking into the pool at others' opinions may cause one to reflect on his or her own opinion, but that reflection is individual and not collective. Polyphonic dialogue is not aimed at aggregating different beliefs, but at constructing a collective understanding necessary for moral insight. Buber writes, "Wouldn't the [statesmen's] world come crashing down upon them if they refused to add up He + He + He to get an It, and tried instead to determine the sum of You and You and You, which can never be anything else than You?" (Buber 1970: 96). Buber here notes the, sometimes subtle, difference between self-actualized view 'He +He = It' versus the relational view 'You and You is a You'.

The relational view of knowledge is concerned not only with the self and the other, but also with the relationship that exists between them. The relational self says, "I will share knowledge in a way that you and I can construct together a new understanding that is at once mine and yours, but also ours." In this sense, the self and the other both see each other as a 'you' (that is to say a *real* person). The 'our' knowledge they gather together comes from "real argumentation and negotiation," making the sum a 'you' (the result of a relationship between two *real* people). Only in the relational view is there an honest effort to focus on agreement rather than a mere accumulation of different perspectives.

The process of constructing collective meaning is part of, but not this entire task. Although Sally and Ed have worked to understand each other's real positions, if their dialogue ends where I have left it, the discussion will remain polarized. Sally and Ed must also share knowledge, in an attempt at least, to reach some common ground.

As stated previously, polarization is a result of contrast-oriented dialogue that begins from difference and disagreement rather than common ground; one is *for* abortion or *against* abortion; one is *for* the death penalty or *against* the death penalty; one is either *for* school prayer or *against* school prayer. Like the characterization of people that is caused by contrast-oriented dialogue, there is also a characterization of opinion that distorts its substantive content. Returning to Ed and Sally's discussion, one can see that using dialogue for self or other, but not for the benefit of the relationship, distorts knowledge and makes polyphonic dialogue impossible. When I left off Sally had said:

> **Sally:** Religion is not like a sport. You do not practice after school, take off your uniform and go home. My religion is my way of life.

Ed now has a choice in responding to Sally. Does he continue to see her as against him and put forth his own beliefs, or does he take a different approach? Martin Buber calls decisions such as the one Ed faces, "walking the narrow ridge." On one hand, Ed firmly believes that prayer should not be allowed in school. On the other hand, Ed is reasonable and he sees that Sally is unveiling her differences, not merely to refute him, but with hopes that he will understand her position. At this moment, Ed is walking the narrow ridge between self and other. Buber writes, "When we walk our way and encounter a man who comes toward us, walking his way, we know our way only and not his; for his comes to life for us only in the encounter" (Buber 1970: 124) Sally and

Ed have made steps toward *real* dialogue, but they have not yet "encountered" one another. Ed is still "walking his way," he is *using* the dialogue to affirm his position. In constructing collective meaning with Sally he has moved closer to an encounter but has not yet entered one.

Envisioning Ed and Sally entering into an encounter with one another involves thinking about dialogue as something that employs and strengthens one's cognitive flexibility. Ed can only really listen to Sally if he is willing to first acknowledge that there are differences between them and then make an attempt to understand not only her opinions, but the reasons she has as a *real* person to believe them. To do this, Ed must choose to relate to, rather than oppose Sally.

Relating does not suppress one's right to argue for one's own position. Arguing one's own position is not a problem unless there is no attempt made to accommodate information and no concern for the relationship with the other. This occurs in adversarial arguments that view the other as an opponent, focusing on disagreement and seeing the other as completely detached from the self. Categorizing information into a *for* and *against* model is a result of *choosing* to take the adversarial outlook toward dialogue. Supporters of adversarial arguments claim that this is a natural form of communication that arises when people or associations have different conceptions of the good. Hearing both sides of the story, supporters say, is fair because everyone has a voice. Listeners hear reasons from both sides (poles) of the argument to help them shape their opinions on the subject.

Among other problems, that I will discuss later, here again one can see the problem of the opinion pool. However many reasons each side gives *for* and *against,* one still sees only a pool full of knowledge piled up. Moral insight does not come from this type of accumulation. Relational exchanges of knowledge are necessary if any collective goal is going to be reached. Even if the people participating in the rally had been focused on listening to each other's positions, this listening would have been shallow. With this in mind, I will now return to Ed and the narrow ridge.

Ed firmly believes that prayer should not be allowed in school. He wants to make his point to Sally sound reasonable, but at the same time he hopes to persuade her. One's desire to persuade the other is not in itself destructive to the dialogue. Again, it is the way one makes his or her point, and not one's position itself, that degrades relationships and polarizes dialogue. To further explore this, I will pose different types of arguments that often monopolize political discussions. These types of arguments polarize and use dialogue to distort the knowledge being offered by self and other. I will then discuss another approach Ed can take, while holding onto his convictions, which allows him to foster a relationship with Sally and enter into an encounter, making moral insight a real possibility.

Shock value arguments make abrupt claims that tend to draw emotional responses because of their force and severity. Making a shock value argument, Ed could say, "You are trying to force your religion on others by arguing for school prayer." These arguments are used to polarize dialogue, instantly compelling the other to take a combative stance. Shock value arguments elicit attention, as the ralliers chanting, "Anti-Zionism is anti-Semitism," knew well; however, these types of overstatements lead to more frustration than insight. Shock value arguments rely on inflated claims rather than reason. Although they may have the advantage of instantly getting others to listen, this listening has nothing to do with the aim of collective understanding.

Snowball arguments can have more merit than shock value arguments because they have a sense of reasoning to them. Snowball or 'What next?' arguments often offer evidence for the path of harms they predict. These arguments can be general, appealing to public moral devolvement, or particular, claiming that individuals will bear the burden of 'bad' policy decisions. For example, a particular snowball argument would be, "If we allow school prayer then students will be drawing attention to their religion. Intolerance will result and religious students may get made fun of for practices that the other students aren't used to." The problem with snowball arguments is not the absence of reasoning, but the distortion of it. The snowball argument is a blueprint of failure, not an attempt at achieving common good. Although it is important to consider possible negative effects of implementing policies, what would ever be resolved if focus was placed solely on failure? Allowing prayer in school may lead to overly religious classrooms or intolerance among students, but making a snowball argument for the other side, not allowing prayer could degrade value-systems and destroy the religious lives of students. An overemphasis on what next and what-ifs does not lead to policy solutions, it only leads to a misrepresentation of policy aims and a movement away from reasonable, relational exchanges of knowledge.

Shifting arguments draw attention to something indirectly related or not at all related to the topic. Shifting arguments move focus away from the topic at hand in order to either affirm one's position, to degrade the other's, or to degrade the dialogue itself by appealing to some external issue. Sometimes arguments move from primary to secondary issues in a way that can be helpful to the dialogue. This kind of shift is not a problem unless one is purposefully shifting the argument in order to avoid addressing the primary issue. The real problem comes from arguments that shift away from the primary issue to another, completely separate issue. An example of this would be, "School prayer is one thing, now the board does not want to open schools until 11:00am so that students can watch the World Cup matches." There may of course be some way to link the primary and shift argument, but that does not help one's aim, which is to engage in a polyphonic dialogue that focuses on common ground that the self and other share.

Another common practice in political dialogue that distorts knowledge and leads to failed relationships is the use of *false analogies*. Analogies can help clarify complicated information when used correctly. However, *false* analogies create confusion and disrupt dialogue. They are often used to overemphasize a point or to manipulate information so that it fits one's position. A false analogy regarding school prayer could be, "Not allowing school prayer is like locking up church doors for half the day." It is important to know how to detect false analogies in arguments. If they go unnoticed, false evidence can dominate an argument.

In addition to these argumentative methods, there are semantic tactics used in political discussions as well. Words have different connotations and intensities. One is capable of completely altering the effect of a statement by his or her choice of words. Two statements with the same literal meaning can have an entirely different influence on the relationship. Certain words and expressions have the capacity to invoke intense reactions without adding any substantive content to their claim. Consider the difference between the claims (1) It's ridiculous that you would consider supporting such an atrocious policy; and (2) I do not understand why you support such a poor policy. Claim (1) polarizes the self from the other by using language that is combative; claim (2) while still voicing disagreement, invites the other to offer reasons for his or her position.

These semantic and argumentative methods stem from adopting an adversarial approach to dialogue that views political discussions as something one can 'win.' If one persuades his or her opponent, then his or her position is affirmed. Even if during the discussion one is careful to listen, comprehend, and be fair-minded, so long as the overall view of the dialogue is something that can be used to win the other over to one's side, the dialogue has failed before it has even begun. As discussed earlier, the self-affirmation view of knowledge is not enough. The focus of *real* political discussions must rest on a concern for both self and other such that relationships can form and encounters can be made possible. Following procedures to listen, comprehend, and be fair-minded require *real* relationships if they are going to help make moral insight possible.

Now I can return to Ed and the narrow ridge. How can Ed hold onto his convictions and enter into an encounter with Sally? All Ed has to do is place his concern for the other (Sally) and the relationship over his desire to 'win' the argument. He has to find out Sally's reasons for her position and have the cognitive flexibility necessary to test them against his own. Here is an example of how Ed could approach Sally:

> **Ed:** I see what you are saying. I am not asking that religious students pretend that they are not religious during the school day. It just seems that there must be a way to work around the school day and have time for prayer.

Here Ed has held on to his position but has made it clear to Sally that he is concerned for her position. The language and argumentative method he has used do not oppose Sally, but rather invite her to continue the discussion. Whether or not Ed is persuaded that there should be school prayer, or Sally is persuaded that there need not be time allotted for it, both of them have encountered each other and fostered a relationship in which the knowledge they share is part of a polyphonic dialogue, making moral insight a real possibility.

As of now this analysis has been centered on the relational failures that result from stressing the importance of difference rather than commonality. The discussion has been focused on the polarization of positions in dialogue. Polarization can occur in large groups as well as between two individuals like Sally and Ed. In America, for example, much of politics is polarized due to the two party system the country ascribes to. However, relational failures do not only result from a polarization of positions. They also occur when a faction of a group is marginalized, isolating the majority from the minority. The three causes of marginalization that I will discuss are race/gender, language, and status/expertise.

Race and gender polarize dialogue when participants are marginalized as a result of personal biases or stereotypes that get in the way of fostering relationships. If Ed, along with a few others had entered into dialogue with Sally holding onto preconceptions about Muslims, Sally's participation would have been controlled or distorted by the other's preexisting beliefs. Becoming stuck in stereotypes is a result of one's failure to accommodate. One cannot expect to get rid of all his or her stereotypes, but one must be able to reexamine generalizations when new information that challenges existing schema is presented. If one has proper concern for the other as a *real* person and shares knowledge for the benefit of relationship, stereotypes and biases will begin to dissolve. The first step toward this is achieving collective meaning. As participants work to create collective meaning and dissolve stereotypes, polyphonic dialogue becomes a real possibility.

Neil Mercer writes, "People offering new and interesting ideas to members of a community, but doing so in ways that do not respond to the communicative ground rules of the communities, may find that their ideas are ignored or rejected simply because they are not presented in the right kind of language" (Mercer 2000: 115). Here Mercer discusses one way in which polarization results when language is used to marginalize dialogue participants. Ideas that are offered in a 'language' that the majority does not speak—whether one literally speaks a different language, has an accent or alternate speech style—his or her ideas are not listened to with the same comprehension and fair-mindedness that is exhibited to other members of the group. When participating in diverse dialogues, it is necessary that one make the effort to give everyone an equal amount of attention. If one has concern for others as *real* people and sees their voice as an important contribution to a polyphonic, intersubjective dialogue, this problem will become less detrimental to political discussions.

Status and expertise polarize a dialogue when jargon is used and the ego-centric view of knowledge is prevalent. Buber writes, "Jargon divides into us and them," either one understands or one does not (Buber 1970: 15). If one does not understand, his or her participation in the dialogue is limited. Those who use jargon and are reluctant to work with others to build collective meaning, tend to hoard knowledge, to use it for self-affirming purposes and to keep those who do not understand marginalized so that they cannot have much influence over the dialogue. Technical language has its place within communities that use the same expert-speech. However, when trying to relate to a diversity of people, it is important to speak in a language that everyone can understand or at least help one another to understand.

I have discussed the force of polarization throughout this paper. I have shown that the only way to follow procedural guidelines is to foster dialogical relationships in order to engage in polyphonic dialogues. In accord with Habermas, I believe focus should be placed on form and procedure in order for moral insight to become a real possibility. In order to truly understand what *real* dialogue entails, one must have concern for self and other, meaning must be seen as something collective, and the relational view of knowledge must be adopted. Once one can achieve this, one can encounter the other as a real person and engage in polyphonic dialogue, making moral insight possible.

It would be easy to look at what has been presented and deem it impossible. Just as a procedure stating one should listen cannot make one listen, how can an outline for what it means to be in a real relationship make that relationship possible? In response to this objection I would like to make two final points. First, this discussion is not meant to solve global conflicts or change political systems. The aim of this analysis is to present a picture of what deliberative dialogues would look like and how they could be made possible taking into account fundamental aspects of the human condition and its tendency toward failed relationships. Secondly, what makes the ideas in this discussion capable of moving from theoretical to practical is the personal quality of their objectives. I do not ask that one attempts to envision a country of people re-conceiving of their relationship with others. Rather, I ask one to be aware of the way he or she interacts with the other; that one make the effort, where possible, to form relationships and enter encounters; that one give up the constant need for self-affirmation and the desire to win and focus instead on building collective meaning and exchanging knowledge in such a way that makes moral insight a real possibility.

Note:

* Ms. Feigenbaum won an award for the best paper presentation at the PPL Honors Conference.

I would like to extend my appreciation to my faculty advisors, Professors Bat-Ami Bar On and Christopher Knapp. I would also like to thank Professor Scalet for this opportunity, as well as Rachel Baskin, Elena Tenenbaum, Christin Wolf, Madelaine Hackett, Greg Sutton, Kevin Leahey, and Professor John Arthur, who helped make this possible.

Works Cited

Arnett, Ronald (1986). *Communication and Community: The Implications of Martin Buber's Dialogue.* Carbondal: Southern Illinois UP.

Buber, Martin (1970) *I and Thou.* Walter Kaufmann (trans.) New York: Scribner.

Festestein, Matthew (1999). "Toleration and Deliberative Politics" in John Horton and Susan Mendus (eds.) *Toleration, Identity, and Difference.* London: McMillan Press Ltd., 146-162.

Freeman, Samuel (2000). "Deliberative Democracy: A Sympathetic Comment". *Philosophy & Public Affairs.* Vol 29, no. 4, ??.

Hacking, Ian (1975). *Why Does Language Matter to Philosophy?* Cambridge; Cambridge UP.

Kymlicka, Will (1995). *Multicultural Citizenship.* Oxford: Oxford UP.

Levy, David A (1997). *Tools of Critical Thinking: Metathoughts for*

Psychology. Needham Heights: Allyn & Bacon.

Mercer, Neil (2000). *Words and Minds.* London: Routledge.

Rawls, John (1997). "Public Reason Revisited" in James Bohman and William Rehg (eds.) *Deliberative Democracy*. Cambridge: MIT Press

Sandel, Michael J. (1996) *Democracy's Discontent: America in Search of a Public Philosophy.* Cambridge: Harvard UP.

Sidorkin, Alexander M. (1999). *Beyonde Discourse: Education, the Self and Dialogue.* Albany: SUNY Press.

Abstract

How should rape be tried? What standards should be used to determine whether or not a person is a rapist? In this paper I argue that, within the confines of heterosexual female acquaintance rape, current standards of determining whether a woman has been raped are inadequate and that an unfair onus continues to be placed on women. I propose a standard of reasonableness involving the discovery as to whether or not a rapist substituted the authoritative voice of the woman with another voice (such as societal convention), thereby replacing her refusal with consent in his mind. I compare this standard with other standards which have been used by courts, and provide an historic overview of rape law reform, as well as an overview of how rape is treated today both inside and outside the courtroom.

STATE V. THE BIG BAD WOLF

AN ANALYSIS OF THE LEGAL TREATMENT OF RAPE

Jonathan Turbin

The idea of rape evokes moral revulsion and outrage. Whether it is an aversion to physical violation or the disregard of a person's autonomy, strong emotions have always come into play when discussing rape.

Despite the moral outrage that accompanies the idea of rape, the crime is still vastly underreported, in part due to the stigma that accompanies rape victims. This stigma that only "certain" women get raped is one of the reasons rape victims are often unwilling to report the crime (Taslitz 1999). Dating back to the seventeenth century, Lord Chief Justice Matthew Hale stated that rape is a charge "easily to be made and hard to be proved, and harder to be defended by the party accused, tho' never so innocent" (Hale 1971).[1] Consequently, it was very difficult for a woman to prove that she had in fact been raped. Up until the middle of the twentieth century American courts were willing to go out of their way to shield male rape defendants (Estrich 1987). Fortunately, there has been much improvement since the days of Lord Hale. The resistance requirement, mandating that there must be evidence of substantial physical resistance on the part of women, has been virtually eliminated, and spousal exclusion, which protects husbands from rape accusations, has been declared unconstitutional. Also, women are technically protected from prejudicial and humiliating intrusions into their private lives at rape trials (Estrich 2000). Rape trial proceedings still have a ways to go, however. For example, women are not always actually protected from questions concerning their sexual past. The purpose of this paper is threefold. First, it aims to give an overview of the act of rape and how it is currently treated by the law (since the two are not the same). Second, it aims to provide an historical overview of the evolution of rape law and how it has changed over time. Its final purpose is to provide an analysis of the legal standard of "reasonableness" in the context of rape law and argue for a change in this standard.

I) Rape and Its Treatment by Law

Rape is defined by U.S. law as "sexual intercourse with another person: (1) by forcible compulsion; (2) Who is incapable of consent by reason of being physically helpless; (3) Who is less than eleven years old" (Penal Law, sec. 130.30). Forcible compulsion is defined as "to compel by either (a) use of physical force; (b) a threat, express or implied, which places a person in fear of immediate death or physical injury to himself, herself or another person, or in fear that he, she or another person will immediately be kidnapped" (ibid). Proving that an alleged rapist used forcible compulsion in order to have sex with his victim is an important element in establishing mens rea. "Mens rea" means guilty mind, meaning in legal discourse that the criminal, in this case the rapist, intended to commit the crime (although, depending on the statute, "recklessness" or "negligence" may also constitute "mens rea"). Mens rea is distinct from "actus reus," which is the criminal act itself; in this case, the actual rape. An important element in establishing the mens rea of a rapist, is whether the accused rapist reasonably believed that the victim consented to sex. The exertion of forcible compulsion bears a direct relationship to mens rea. This is because forcible compulsion used to overcome resistance indicates an intent to have sex with or without one's partner's consent.

There are two classes of rape: aggravated and simple rape. These terms were coined by Professors Harry Kalven and Hans Zeisel of the University of Chicago in the mid-1960s during their study of American juries (Estrich 1987). Aggravated rape includes cases where there is no prior relationship between the victim and the attacker. Simple rape is rape by an acquaintance. It is rape by a significant other (used here to mean a lover or spouse), a date, a friend, a coworker, or a casual acquaintance. Simple rape is far more difficult to prosecute, for reasons which will be explained (ibid).

This difficulty arises from the reaction simple rape elicits from society. Due to the physical and psychological trauma that accompanies rape, most women do not acknowledge the fact that rape can happen to them. Therefore, victims of simple rape tend to deny to themselves that they have even been raped. Also, it is commonly thought that rape only happens to women who are "loose," foolish, uneducated, or unstable. Likewise the crime of rape is typically thought of as a crime perpetrated in a back alley by an unshaven stranger with a weapon, or in a scary forest by the big bad wolf. However, rape survivors can be anyone from college students, to attorneys, to teachers, to homemakers. According to a 1990 hearing in the United States House of Representatives, 15 to 40 percent of women believe themselves to have been victims of attempted or completed rape at some point during their lives (U.S. House 1990). Also, according to the same hearing, 50 to 70 percent of all rapes happen within the context of an ongoing relationship. Rapists are not readily identifiable as "bad guys", but it is common for them to rape again if not apprehended (ibid).

The reaction of police to simple rape victims has a significant effect as well. Nancy Madigan and Lee Gamble, authors of "The Second Rape," interviewed twenty-four police officers in Southern California and discovered trends which they believe are general attitudes of police throughout the United States. While many public safety servants are committed, they are also overworked and do not have the time to focus all their energy on one particular case. Also, not all police officers are experienced with the crime of rape, nor have they been exposed to rape victims. For example, 50 to 70 percent of initial responses to 911 rape calls are handled by police rookies with little exposure to such complaints outside the academy. This is in addition to the countless other new problems a rookie must deal with (Madigan and Gamble 1991). I believe that this is a problem because the police are often the first people a woman turns to when she has been raped.

Even if the police officer has dealt with rape cases before, she or he may still have a negative impact on the rape victim. In Madigan and Gamble's study, they found that an officer may have certain attitudes about rape that will lead her or him to abandon a case. Since in such a situation they are not open to public attacks, the officer may do this quietly. While screening rape cases, the police assess the victim's credibility. She must articulate the events which occurred before, during, and after the event. It must be cogent and chronological. If alcohol or drugs played any part, her story is immediately suspect. The investigator also intrudes on the most personal intimate details of the victim's life, a situation which is humiliating. It seems that the police screen cases based on the archaic notion that only "certain women" are rape victims (ibid). I believe that making a woman's morals an issue serves to perpetuate the practice of blaming the victim.

Along these lines, police have adopted the concept of the "victim-precipitated" rape. Menachem Amir, a sociologist who studied Philadelphia rape cases in 1958 and 1960, adopted this term. He considered rapes to be "victim precipitated" if the woman acted in a way that could possibly be interpreted as a sexual invitation — having a drink with a man, accepting or offering him a ride, leaving a party with him or working late with him. In effect, Menachem Amir concludes his study by asserting that most rape victims should have known better, and that this does not really make their assailants culpable (Estrich 1987). Poor judgment on the part of the rape victim is a very common rationale, mirroring the attitudes of society. Perhaps there are some instances where a woman "should have known better." However, intuition tells me that the horrible experience of a rape is far too gruesome a punishment for accepting a ride from a strange man or walking alone in a bad part of town. Furthermore, the rapist is hardly the person to issue the punishment for so-called lack of judgment.

Professor Amir's conclusion, whether valid or invalid, is apparently shared by many juries. In the study of American juries by Professors Harry Kalven and Hans Zeisel (discussed supra, p.3), it was found that juries tend to be exceedingly lenient with defendants if there is any evidence of possibly contributory behavior on the part of the victim (Madigan and Gamble 1991).

Another fact taken into account by police investigators is the level of resistance displayed by the rape victim. This level of resistance is important to the investigator because it is used to determine whether the accused knew he was using forcible compulsion: that is, whether he had mens rea. Recent laws have lowered the threshold of what constitutes forcible compulsion, however, old attitudes about resistance tend to remain. Even today, a victim must assertively communicate her non-consent. Also, physical injuries resulting from physical resistance still make a case much stronger. Non-consent in the form of a verbal "no" or a struggle unaccompanied by significant physical injuries, on the whole have little weight with police, and in particular with juries, who still tend to adhere to the old idea that a woman who faces the possibility of rape must resist to the utmost of her ability. Many people still believe the notion of "death before dishonor" when it comes to female virtue (taken to mean chastity) (ibid).

This stringent attitude on the part of jurors towards rape cases has a heavy influence on potential prosecutors. Prosecutors tend to decide which cases to take based on virtually identical criteria used by the police: prior relationships with the accused, previous sexual history, personal manner, etc. Susan Estrich describes her experience with a seemingly "liberal" public prosecutor in her book *Real Rape*. An attractive young woman walked into his office wanting to file rape charges against her ex-boyfriend. According to her story, she ran into her former boyfriend on the street. He invited her up to his apartment and they started watching a movie. He started kissing her and she got up to leave. He pulled her onto the bed and forced himself on her. She did not resist because he was a weightlifter, so she had no bruises. The prosecutor turned her down because, according to him, in such a case it would be impossible to get a conviction. The fact that the rapist in question was not a "bad guy" did not help matters.

Ironically, the prosecutor told Estrich that if the woman's story was true, she was in fact raped. The prosecutor did not take the case because it was not the kind of case, given the details the woman provided in her story, he was likely to win. Estrich writes that the only unusual thing about the circumstances here are that the woman, a victim of simple rape, decided to prosecute. The decision on the part of the prosecutor to turn her down was not (Estrich 1987).

Moving on from the police, courts, and prosecutors, this paper will now discuss actual law. Again, there have been drastic improvements in American rape law. Courts are far more likely now, than in the past, to see a man's conduct as rape if a woman says "no" and attempts some physical resistance as opposed to the old requirement of showing utmost resistance. However, verbal resistance is still not sufficient to bring legal safeguards into play, due to the old idea that when a woman says "no" she sometimes means "yes." Even today, most states still have no law requiring courts, or potential sexual partners, to accept a negative verbal statement at face value (Schulhofer 1998).

II) Attempts at Law Reform in the Late 20th Century

While much has fortunately changed since the time of Lord Hale, many courts still remain suspicious of female victims of simple rape, and are protective of male defendants. Now, force or threat of force is used in lieu of resistance to the utmost, or as corroborating testimony and evidence in order to prove non-consent. However, I believe that this reform, which supposedly focuses on the amount of force used by the accused, has been undercut by the fact that the degree of force is still measured by the amount of resistance put forth by the victim.

A striking example of this is *State v. Alston*, a 1984 decision by the North Carolina Supreme Court. Alston had been involved in a "consensual" relationship with the victim. This relationship involved some violence on the part of the defendant and passivity on the part of the victim (1984). After the termination of their relationship, Alston went to the victim's school, accosted her, and blocked her path. He grabbed her arm and stated that she was coming with him. They walked and talked about their relationship. At one point Alston declared that he was going to "fix" her face to show he "was not playing." When she told him that their relationship was over, Alston insisted that he had a "right" to have intercourse with her again. The two of them went to a house of a friend of the defendant. The defendant asked if she was "ready." The victim stated she did not want to have intercourse. Alston undressed her, pushed her down on a bed, pushed her legs apart, and penetrated her. She did not use physical resistance, but did cry during the act (ibid).

After being convicted by a jury, the North Carolina Supreme Court reversed Alston's conviction. While holding that a rape victim does not have to offer physical resistance and finding that the victim in this case clearly did not consent, the court held that there was a lack of substantial evidence that the accused used force. The victim had not resisted physically, and her failure to resist was not a result of what the defendant had done prior to penetration. The fact that Alston grabbed the victim's arm and threatened to "fix her face" may have caused her fear, but they were unrelated to the sexual intercourse. The court found that most of the woman's fears were based on her prior experience with the relationship, and deemed it irrelevant. "Although [the victim's] general fear of the defendant may have been justified by his conduct on prior occasions, absent evidence that the defendant used force or threats to overcome the will of the victim to resist the sexual intercourse alleged to have been rape, such general fear was not sufficient to show that the defendant used the force required to support a conviction of rape." The undressing and pushing of legs apart were not even mentioned by the court (ibid).

There is, in my mind at least, a contradiction in terms here (Susan Estrich makes a similar assertion in *Real Rape*). The court stated that consent was not at issue. It also said there was no force. Therefore, the woman was not forced to engage in sex (as proven by her failure to resist), yet the sex was against her will. I do not find it difficult to see how anyone who had been physically abused repeatedly during a relationship with someone who subsequently confronts and threatens her, and then summons the courage which is not innate in her to tell him that the relationship is over, only to be answered by an assertion of a "right" to sex, would not fight his advances. This is the reaction of people who have already been beaten. During the rape, Alston did not beat his victim; he did not need to. She had been beaten by him, physically and emotionally, months before. Unlike a woman's previous sexual experiences, which are irrelevant because they have no bearing on her consent, the previous experience of the victim in *Alston* in an abusive relationship was relevant, for the above reasons. However, the court failed to recognize this.

People v. Evans is another relevant case. In this 1975 New York case, an "incredibly gullible" college sophomore found herself in a threatening situation. Evans told the woman that he was a psychologist conducting an experiment. He convinced her to come to an apartment he claimed to use as an office. After she rejected his advances, he said: "Look where you are. You are in the apartment of a strange man. How do you know that I am really who I say I am? How do you know that I am really a psychologist . . . I could kill you. I could rape you. I could hurt you physically." He then forced himself on her. The trial court found him "reprehensible," and his "seduction" was "conquest by con job." But it was not criminal. The court found Evans' words to be ambiguous; capable of being either a threat or the chiding of a foolish girl. His conduct was labeled "seduction," and the trial court declared "men on the make, fear not. It is still not illegal to feed a girl a line, to continue the attempt, not to take no for a final answer, at least not the first time . . . Every man is free, under the law, to be a gentleman or a cad" (1975). Since people who chide the foolish seldom force themselves upon the foolish, I believe the court's judgment was in error. Evan's statement was a threat, and therefore his conduct was a rape.

An even more sinister case was the 1984 Pennsylvania decision, *Commonwealth v. Mlinarich*. In this case the Pennsylvania Superior Court defined "forcible compulsion" as the key element of the state's rape law. However, "physical compulsion or violence" did not include "psychological duress." In this case the victim was Mlinarich's fourteen-year-old legal ward. He threatened to return her to a detention home if she did not agree to have intercourse with him. Under the court's definition, the defendant's actions were reprehensible, but they were not rape. The law did not equate seduction, "benign or sinister, with rape." Since seduction was not a crime, there was no crime in these instances (1985). Indeed, in these cases seduction is given a wide berth. Had Mr. Mlinarich threatened to send the victim to reform school unless he was paid off with money, he might well have been guilty of extortion. Therefore, the fact that Mlinarich demanded sex as a payoff should have warranted a conviction.

The history of rape law was grounded in Lord Hale's fear that, short of injuries resulting from struggling with her attacker, there was no way to be sure a woman was not "crying rape." A rape victim's truthfulness has always been in question, as she was often suspected of covering an illicit pregnancy, hiding an affair, or seeking revenge for a suddenly terminated relationship. The "male rape fantasy" — the fear men tend to have of being dragged through rape trial proceedings by a lying and vindictive woman — has heavily influenced rape law through the ages (Taslitz 1999).

III) Once Upon a Time: A History of Rape Law

At its earliest stages, the law embraced the concept of "death before dishonor" with regard to rape law. Female non-consent needed to be demonstrated not merely by some degree of physical struggle, but by what was termed "utmost resistance" (Tomaselli and Porter 1986). I disagree with this tactic, as I believe it is the most efficient way to blame the victim. I shall attempt to prove so below.

The concept of "utmost resistance" is starkly illustrated in *Brown v. State,* a 1906 Wisconsin decision and subsequent appeal. It is also the epitome of a simple rape.

The victim in Brown, a sixteen-year-old woman was a neighbor and childhood friend of the twenty-year-old Brown. She testified at trial that as she was walking to her grandmother's house along the meadow adjoining their houses, she greeted Brown. He grabbed her, tripped her, and raped her. According to the victim " [I] tried as hard as I could to get away. I was trying all the time to get away just as hard as I could. I was trying to get up; I pulled at the grass; I screamed as hard as I could, and he told me to shut up, and I didn't, and then he held his hand on my mouth until I was almost strangled." The jury found the defendant guilty (1906).

The Supreme Court of Wisconsin, however, reversed Brown's conviction on appeal. It did not state that Brown's force was insufficient to successfully complete the rape, nor did it assert that he lacked the criminal mindset, or mens rea. However, the court claimed that the victim had not adequately demonstrated non-consent. In addition to a complete mental and verbal refusal, there must be " . . . vehement exercise of every physical means or faculty within the woman's power to resist the penetration of her person . . ." (ibid). As for the young woman in *Brown*, her resistance was not enough. "Her outer clothing not only presented no tearing, but no disarray, so far as the testimony goes. When one pauses to reflect upon the *terrific resistance which the determined woman should make, such a situation is well-nigh incredible* . . . We are convinced that there was no evidence of the resistance which is essential to the crime of rape . . ." (ibid). [my emphasis] The words of the *Brown* court reveal that they viewed utmost resistance as merely the natural response of any good woman to unwanted sex.

The rather tragic irony in these cases is that in a society where the proper female role was passive and powerless, women were expected to be aggressive and powerful in matters of resisting sex. Likewise, while chastity on the part of women was celebrated, the legal system tended to err on the side of female consent. Courts granted men very broad sexual access to the women they knew, which proved punitive to rape victims.

Nonetheless, the standard of "utmost resistance" was at times applied selectively (Estrich 1987). In a farsighted decision in 1886, the Virginia Supreme Court decided to waive the utmost resistance requirement in *Bailey v. Commonwealth*. In this case, Bailey was the 14-year-old victim's infatuated stepfather. One night, the defendant went home and entered the girl's bedroom. "She forbid his getting into the bed, but he got in. She said she would tell her mother, and he said, 'If you do, I will whip you.'" She " . . . made no further resistance." The court acknowledged the rule that, "though she objects verbally, if she makes no outcry and no resistance, she by her conduct consents, and the carnal act is not rape in the man." Bailey's conviction was affirmed, however: "Should *he* be permitted to shelter himself behind the circumstance that she made but little actual resistance, and no outcry, under circumstances to her, so confusing and so intimidating? There he was, one in authority, standing over her . . . That she *felt* herself in his power, and took too much counsel of her fears . . . is a matter that he cannot plead in extenuation of his crime" (1886). [emphasis in original] I believe that this was the proper decision since the man didn't need to overpower his stepdaughter or draw a gun on her in order to justify a conviction.

The Virginia Supreme Court found other cases which justified the waiving of the "utmost resistance" rule. The attempted rape of a "simple, good, unsophisticated country girl" who happened to be white by a black man was taken to justify the death penalty, with the court never once suggesting that "utmost exertion" be required (Hart v. the Commonwealth 1921). By the same token, however, when a black man was convicted of the rape of a black women whom, the court noted, was unwed with two children, the Virginia Supreme Court ordered a reversal of conviction: "The evidence indicates that he had wooed her pretty roughly in a way that would have been . . . a shocking outrage toward a woman of virtuous sensibilities . . . But how far it affected the sensibilities of the prosecutrix does not appear. It by no means appears . . . that it was an attempt to . . . overcome her virtue, which had yielded to others before . . ." (Christian v. the Commonwealth 1873). As has often been done with rape cases, the victim's personal conduct has, wrongly, been made an issue.

According to Bat-Ami Bar On in her essay "The "Scottsboro Case:" On Responsibility, Rape, Race, Gender, and Class," these two differing decisions are auspicious. " . . . the good/bad and rapable/unrapable distinctions racialize women because of the clustering of goodness, rapeability and Whiteness on one side and badness, unrapability and Blackness on the other" (Bar On in Burgess-Jackson 1999). It seems that it is not only womanly virtue and manly force which is to be taken into account; the "appropriateness of the relationship must be as well. The black stranger raping a white woman is at one end of the spectrum, with partners in marriage being the most appropriate relationship possible. In between these two benchmarks are variant degrees of 'appropriateness.' Strangers are 'inappropriate;' they need not be resisted, but dates must be. A stepdaughter needn't resist her stepfather, but she must resist her male next-door neighbor. White women don't have to resist black men, but black women must. The broadened sexual access the resistance requirement allowed only applied in 'appropriate relationships'" (Estrich 1987). I believe that this standard of appropriateness, informally but firmly imposed by courts does not do equal justice to rape complainants.

By 1950, the standard of "reasonable resistance" began to replace the "utmost resistance" requirement. Judges no longer held that chastity was more important than life itself. While a positive change, it did not go far enough. The legal literature of the 1950s and 1960s still questioned victims of simple rape because most men believed that women were ambivalent about having sex in "appropriate relationships." According to a 1966 *Stanford Law Review* article:

> Although a woman may desire sexual intercourse, it is customary for her to say, "no, no, no" (although meaning "yes, yes, yes") and to expect the male to be the aggressor . . . It is always difficult in rape cases to determine whether the female really meant "no" . . . The problem of determining what the female "really meant" is compounded when, in fact, the female had no clearly determined attitude — that is, her attitude was one of ambivalence . . . often a woman faces a "trilemma"; she is faced with a choice among being a prude, a tease, or an "easy lay." Furthermore, a woman may note a man's brutal nature

> and be attracted to him rather than repulsed (1966).

Similarly, the 1952 *Yale Law Journal's* article "Forcible and Statutory Rape" cited Freud's theory that while not a habitual liar, the average woman is unsure about having sex with men she knows. Her behavior is not an accurate compass of her true desires, since it may suggest resistance when the woman is really enjoying physically struggling:

> When her behavior looks like resistance although her attitude is one of consent, injustice may be done the man by the woman's subsequent accusation. Many women, for example, require as a part of preliminary "love play" aggressive overtures by the man. Often their erotic pleasure may be enhanced by . . . an accompanying physical struggle. The "love bite" is a common, if mild, sign of the aggressive component in the sex act. And the tangible signs of struggle may survive to support a subsequent accusation by the woman (1952).

The authors conclude that if a woman is ambivalent about sex, therefore it is unfair to punish a man who is not entirely acting contrary to her wishes (ibid).

These legal writings and the cases which reflect them demonstrate a departure from Hale's seventeenth century view that women are vindictive liars towards a belief that the average woman does not know what she wants or does not mean what she says in a sexual situation. Besides, the use of force doesn't really mean anything since a woman enjoys, or perhaps even depends on force for physical pleasure. While the move away from utmost resistance was a good thing, this method was also harmful to rape victims.

IV) Requiring Corroboration for Conviction

As an alternative to utmost resistance, some courts required that the victim's testimony be corroborated by other evidence. The absence of corroborating evidence was at its most critical when the case depended on a question of attitude (that is, the meaning of "no") or where a woman's story was considered to be too incredible to be believed on its own merits alone.

The requirement of victim corroboration was applied in many jurisdictions. The justification was, to put it in layman's terms, that women lie. As the *Columbia Law Review* claimed in the 1960s: "Surely the simplest, and perhaps the most important, reason not to permit conviction for rape on the uncorroborated word of the prosecutrix is that that word is very often false . . . Since stories of rape are frequently lies or fantasies, it is reasonable to provide that such a story, in itself, should not be enough to convict a man of a crime" (1967). While there probably have been some cases where the woman has lied, these cases are not frequent enough to warrant a policy like the corroboration requirement. The ludicrousness of it is demonstrated below.

Similar to reversals of convictions due to the lack of proof of utmost resistance, reversals based on a lack of corroborating evidence tended to occur in simple rape cases. Corroboration of testimony was demanded when there was a lack of proof of utmost resistance.

Take for example the 1894 Minnesota case *State v. Connelly*. In this case the prosecutrix was a seventeen-year-old who claimed that she had been raped by her next door neighbor, a Catholic priest. She also testified that she was pregnant with his child. The court reversed the conviction, concluding that "where the charge is true, there will almost always be some corroborating evidence, such as injury to the person or clothing of the prosecutrix, or the fact that she made complaint as soon as practicable . . . yet even young girls, like older females, sometimes concoct an untruthful story to conceal a lapse from virtue" (1894).

It is this type of case which is addressed by the commentators to the *1980 Model Penal Code,* which called for the retention of the corroboration requirement. Their argument is based on Lord Hale's recognition that it is very hard to defend against a false accusation of sexual offense in cases where the chief question is one of attitude:

> The difference between criminal and noncriminal conduct depends ultimately on a question of attitude. Proof of this elusive issue often boils down to a confrontation of conflicting accounts. The corroboration requirement is an attempt to skew resolution of such disputes in favor of the defendant. It does not, or at least need not, rest on the assertion that one person's testimony is inherently more deserving of credence than another's . . : It is, rather, a determination to favor justice to the defendant, even at some cost to the societal interest in effective law enforcement and to the personal demands of the victim for redress. In short, the corroboration requirement should not be understood as an effort to discount female testimony or as an unsympathetic understanding of the female experience with sexual aggression. It is, rather, only a particular implementation of the general policy that uncertainly should be resolved in favor of the accused (1980).

These cases depending "ultimately on a question of attitude" are cases of simple rape. Women involved in simple rape cases find themselves in a sort of Catch-22. Since there are very rarely witnesses to a rape, corroboration usually consists of physical injuries and torn clothing which are signs of physical resistance. Ironically, corroboration was instituted to substitute proof of utmost resistance.

V) A Woman's Past on Trial

In recent years, much controversy has surrounded the practice of questioning a woman about her sexual history. Many courts found evidence of previous un-chastity pertinent to the issue of consent and to the woman's credibility as a witness. I find un-chastity completely irrelevant. No matter how many times a woman consents to sex, it does not mean that she always will. While some courts restricted evidence of relations with men other than the defendant to testimony of general reputation, that is, witnesses could be asked if the victim had a "past," other courts flat out allowed cross-examination and direct evidence of recent sexual encounters. Sometimes the men themselves could be called as witnesses (Estrich 1987).

It has been proven scientifically that questioning a woman about her sexual history has a prejudicial effect on the trier of fact. Sociological studies have shown that there is a direct correlation between how chaste a woman is and how serious her rape is perceived to be. The rape of a sexually experienced woman is viewed as a less serious assault (L'Armond and Pepitone 1982). I find this point of view completely out of line. Rape is traumatic for any person.

In the most typical scenario, the victim will be questioned about her intimacy with men other than the defendant. One such case is *Packineau v. United States*, a 1953 case. This case involved a rape committed on an American Indian nation in North Dakota, thereby bringing it within federal jurisdiction. In this case, two men and two women, all American Indians of around the same age, went for a ride together and drank whiskey. The victim testified that at one point she felt sick and got out of the car for some air. She was followed by one of the defendants who attempted to seduce her and, when she rebuffed him, punched her. As she lay stunned on the ground the second defendant approached her and, according to her testimony, raped her. The first defendant was convicted of aiding and abetting. The second defendant was convicted of rape. These convictions were reversed on appeal, in the first case due to lack of proof of the intent required for aiding and abetting, and the second because of erroneous exclusion of proof of previous un-chastity by the victim with other men. Consent was not at issue here because the defendant denied any act of intercourse. However, the United States Court of Appeals held that evidence of the victim's previous sexual relations must be given because this case did not involve aggravated, stranger-in-the-woods rape:

> It might be that there are cases where a woman has been set upon and forcibly ravished by strangers coming out of ambush or the like and any inquiry as to her chastity or lack of it is irrelevant. But in this case the prosecutrix, as stated in the brief for the government, was "a very refined girl, who attended the school at the Indian Agency and then went to high school and was attending Haskill, the Indian School at Lawrence, Kansas, where she was preparing herself for nurses training." Her appearance and the evidence concerning her antecedents tended to enhance the credibility of her testimony, and to offset unfavorable inferences that might otherwise have been drawn from the part of her night's adventures that were admittedly of her own volition . . . That her story of having been raped would be more readily believed by a person who was ignorant of any former unchaste conduct on her part than it would be by a person cognizant of the unchaste conduct defendants offered to prove against her seems to clear for argument (1953).

The defendant had the right to attack the victim's credibility on the grounds of her previous un-chastity, but it was not allowable for him to be attacked in the same way. The *Packineau* court concluded that "Questioning about his illegitimate family necessarily prejudiced the jury against [him]" (ibid).

Courts are never as willing to allow inquiries into a male defendant's sexual history because of the prejudice which might result. And again, the woman's sexual history, with the defendant and with other men, becomes relevant chiefly in simple rape cases. The Packineau case is significant because it demonstrates how courts have been willing to allow cross-examinations concerning a woman's sexual past, but overly concerned with the prejudicial effects of similar questioning of the defendant.

In a 1929 California case, *People v. Biescar*, the exact same attitude of protecting the defendant and humiliating the victim is adopted. In this case, the defendant had been convicted of raping a woman with whom he had been driving and drinking. His conviction was reversed because the appellate court believed that the trial court should not have allowed cross-examination of him concerning visits by other women to his bachelor pad, but should have allowed cross-examination of the victim concerning a "wild" all-night party she attended a few days earlier (1929).

VI) Fresh Complaint in a Rape Prosecution

The rule of fresh complaint states that "a failure of the assaulted party to make complaint recently after the occurrence, opportunity offering itself, will cast a suspicion on the bona fides of the charge" (Stewart v. State 1932). The absence of a fresh complaint would cause "a strong but not a conclusive presumption against a woman" (Blackstone 1966).

When the Model Penal Code was drafted, there was no blanket barring of prosecution when fresh complaint was lacking. The Code proposed the requirement of a complaint within three months as a prerequisite for prosecution. Several states followed suit. The justification was stated thus: "The requirement of prompt complaint springs in part from a fear that unwanted pregnancy or bitterness at a relationship gone sour might convert a willing participant in sexual relations into a vindictive complainant" (1980).

The fresh-complaint rule reflects the stereotype of the lying, vindictive woman. This rule, according to the court, is "founded upon the laws of human nature. It is so natural as to be almost inevitable that a female upon whom the crime has been committed will make immediate complaint" (State v. Connelly 1894). The truth, however, is far different. Considering the reaction of police, prosecutors, and jurors, a rape victim has every cause to delay in reporting a rape.

VII) Heightened Standard of Proof in a Rape Prosecution

The final example of evidentiary distrust is the cautionary instruction. Juries are always told that, in order to convict, they must be convinced of the defendant's guilt beyond a reasonable doubt. This, apparently, is not enough. In rape cases they have always been told that they must be particularly suspicious of the woman victim. The jury is told to "evaluate the testimony of a victim or complaining witness with special care in view of the emotional involvement of the witness and the difficulty of determining the truth with respect to alleged sexual activities carried out in private" (Model Penal Code and Commentaries 1980).

VIII) Summary

These rules have historically conspired to protect male defendants. The requirement that women resist, strictly applied in non-stranger cases, squarely places the onus on the woman to give men the needed notice that sex is unwelcome. The requirement of corroboration, again applied mainly in simple rape cases, prevents a credibility contest. Fresh complaint limits the freedom of a woman to turn on her former lover after he has spurned her (at least according to the "vindictive woman phobia"). To add insult to injury, the cautionary instruction reminds the jury of the "unfair" position in which the man has found himself to be and the suspicion women supposedly deserve.

IX) *The Impossibility of Conviction in the Most Simple of Simple Rapes, The Marriage Bed*

According to the liberal definition of "seduction" arrived at by the courts in *Mlinarich* and *Evans*, men in appropriate relationships have a broad liberty to seduce. In the most appropriate relationship of all, marriage, husbands traditionally have had the broadest liberty. A husband could use as much coercion as he pleased without fear of a rape charge. Traditionally, within the confines of a marriage, a woman is seen as giving her general, perpetual consent from the moment she says "I do" at the wedding until she signs her name on the divorce papers. To quote Lord Hale again, "The husband cannot be guilty of rape committed by himself upon his lawful wife, for by their mutual matrimonial consent and contract, the wife hath given up herself in this kind unto her husband, which she cannot retract."

Furthermore, sex within a marital relationship is seen as nebulous and ambiguous, and therefore a rape charge lodged by a wife against her husband is thought to be impossible to prove or refute. Additionally, one of the most potent arguments against defining marital rape as a crime is that it will lead to frivolous complaints by angry wives. This is yet another example of the fear of the "vindictive woman" (see p. 11, supra). Finally, like all cases of simple rape, betrayal by an intimate, in this case the most intimate of all intimates, is seen to be not so bad (Finkelhor and Yllo 1985). Again, while much positive progress has been made in this area, as will be discussed below, the law has not come far enough.

Marital rape has been portrayed as relatively innocuous. Usually the husband is seen as having a healthy, if overzealous, sexual appetite, and the wife is repressed or squeamish. Many times the marital rape is portrayed as almost romantic. Albeit most likely not the idea of the director, Filkelhor and Yllo, authors of *License to Rape*, find in the film *Gone with the Wind* a potent image of marital rape. In this movie a "healthy sexual" man, Rhett Butler (Clark Gable) overcomes the resistance of the reluctant Scarlett O'Hara (Vivian Leigh). He carries his struggling wife up Tara's elegant staircase to an outcome tastefully left to the viewer's imagination. The next scene shows Scarlett preening herself the next morning, glowing and giddy. *Gone with the Wind*, according to Finkelhor and Yllo, advertises the idea that rape is an acceptable way to treat one's reluctant wife. It may even be a way to resolve marital disputes (ibid).

As stated by the Colorado Supreme Court in 1981, the marital exemption rule "may remove a substantial obstacle to the resumption of normal marital relations" and also "averts difficult emotional issues and problems of proof inherent in this sensitive area" (Estrich 1987). All in all, if courts find non-consent in a dating relationship too ambiguous to be punished as rape, how much more so in the marriage bed (ibid).

A few state courts have been willing to reject the idea of marital exemption. One of these states, New York, did so in 1984 in *People v. Liberta.* In this case Liberta, a twenty-six year old Buffalo man, was convicted of raping his wife from whom he was separated by a court order of protection. Liberta's attorneys appealed his conviction, arguing that Liberta's right to equal protection of the law was violated because New York State law protected husbands from being prosecuted for raping their wives. In affirming Liberta's conviction, the New York Court of Appeals rejected the marital exemption rule for rape in toto (1984). First, the court recognized that the tradition of spousal exemption lay within the view of wife-as-chattel, a view which had long since been abandoned. Second, the idea that a couple should be protected against government intrusion which could prevent reconciliation was probably erroneous, since there is most likely little hope for reconciliation in a marriage where a rape has taken place. Third, as for the difficulty inherent in discerning the difference between non-consent and a vindictive wife, the court stated that the safeguards inherent in the judicial system are presumed capable of handling false complaints. Finally, the court recognized that marital rape may have consequences equally or more severe than other rapes (Finkelhor and Yllo 1985).

At last, in New York State, it was illegal to rape one's wife. Sadly, however, cases like *Liberta* are the exception rather than the rule, and are not usually prosecuted unless the facts are truly horrific, such as Liberta's vicious brutality towards his wife, and the fact that he raped her in front of their young child (Estrich 1987). I find the fact that men are still protected from prosecution for this heinous act, except in the most extreme of circumstances, to be highly unfortunate.

X) Mens Rea and the "Reasonable Man:" When No Means No

To successfully convict a person of a crime, including rape, two elements must be proven: actus reus and mens rea. Actus reus is the criminal act itself, and mens rea is the criminal intent on the part of the perpetrator. With regard to rape, whether or not the perpetrator reasonably believed that the victim consented to sex is the principle component of mens rea (see p. 2, supra).

David Archard developed a schematic demonstrating the difficulty of establishing mens rea in a simple rape or, in other words, how even if a man believes a woman has consented to sex, his belief may be unreasonable:

(1) Smith had sex with Jones.
(2) At the time of this sex, Jones did not consent to sex with Smith.
(3) Smith would not have had sex with Jones had he believed (2).
(4) At the time of this sex, Smith did not believe (2).
(5) In some sense, it may be appropriate to describe Smith's cognitive state as specified in (4) as unreasonable (Archard in Burgess-Jackson 1999).

A specific case which acts out Archard's schematic is *Director of Public Prosecutions v. Morgan*, an English 1975 case involving a man who convinced a group of young men to have intercourse with his wife. He told them that any expressions of protest on the part of his wife were "playacting," since his wife enjoyed "forced sex." Even though the men believed she was consenting, and would not have had intercourse with her had they known she was not, their state of mind can still be termed unreasonable. This case led the House of Lords to conclude that an honest but unreasonable mistake regarding consent may be used as grounds for acquittal in a rape trial (ibid).

"Mens rea" is basically a guilty or criminal mind, meaning that the intent of a criminal to commit a crime must be proven. In rape, mens rea requires that it be proven that the rapist intended on having intercourse with his victim whether she consented or not. However, what if the accused simply made an honest mistake? In fact, most potential rapists believe that their victims genuinely like them (at least in simple rape). The unreasonable belief of the young men in *Morgan* in the consent of the woman is an example of a rape without clear mens rea (that is, the young men did not set out with intent to rape) (May and Soule in Burgess-Jackson 1999).

Returning to Archard's schematic, taken together, (1) and (2) define the "actus reus" of rape. Smith, a man, had sex with Jones, a woman, to which she did not consent. Statement (3) tells us that Smith does not disregard the importance of Jones' consent. If he knew she was not consenting he would not have sex with her. To quote Lord Hailsham's phrase in the *Morgan* judgment, he does not proceed "willy-nilly not caring whether the victim consents or no" (1975).

Statement (4) defines Smith's mindset. It is important to note that it does not say that Smith necessarily thought Jones was consenting. It merely states that he did not know that she was not. He could have held the belief that she wanted to have sex with him, but he could merely not have given the possibility of her non-consent any thought. Let us assume, however, that he does believe her consent. To decide if the reasons for this belief are reasonable, we must add statement (5) which is determinative as to whether a rape has taken place (Archard in Burgess-Jackson 1999).

There are reasons why a man might think an unconsenting woman is consenting. Smith might not have even considered the fact that Jones might not be consenting. He believes that she does consent by putting out of his mind any consideration that she may not. A belief in consent is based on a lack of belief in non-consent. Another possibility is that Smith considers the possibilities but concludes that she is. Thus he has made an "honest mistake" (ibid).

There are reasonable mistakes men can make regarding non-consent. For example, in the Archard schematic, Jones could correctly believe that there is an escaped psychopath, Brown, who enjoys raping women, especially when he secures sexual compliance from them which could easily be confused with consensual, pleasurable sex. If a woman does not act this out, Brown resorts to brutal violence. Jones erroneously believes Smith is Brown and has sex with him. Smith believes Jones is consenting, and definitely would not have gone through with it had he known otherwise. Jones acquiesces out of terror, but she hides her terror, showing a facade of pleasured compliance. She thinks she must do so in order to prevent "Brown" from detecting her real feelings and brutally retaliating.

In this case (1) through (4) are true, but we can hardly call Smith's belief in consent unreasonable. It seems that neither he nor any other reasonable person can doubt that Jones' behavior reflected genuine consent. Should Smith have asked Jones "are you making me think that you really consent to sex with me because you actually think I am the psychopath Brown?" How should Jones answer this if she still thinks that Smith is Brown? Thus a man can make a reasonable mistake regarding consent and non-consent, illustrating point number (5) in the schematic, requiring an examination of the cognitive state of the accused to see whether his belief in consent was reasonable or not. Obviously, in some way, Jones must make it clear that she does not want to have sex with Smith (ibid).

Mistakes regarding the particulars of a sexual encounter are very common. Men have been led to believe that their male sexual partner is a woman, and often are convinced feigned orgasms are genuine. Thus the most significant kind of mistake, consent is no exception. In *Morgan* several men, sincerely if unreasonably, mistook signs of physical resistance for complicit pleasure in consensual sex (Burgess-Jackson in Burgess-Jackson 1999).

If it is possible to be mistaken about another's consent, what then makes certain mistakes unreasonable? It must be borne in mind that the mistaken belief is not necessarily an insincere one. An unreasonable belief may be firmly and sincerely adhered to. In order to truly evaluate the reasonableness of a belief, one first must evaluate the consequences of being mistaken. This is especially important in terms of consent.

Second, the value of that which is being risked by holding the belief must be evaluated. In the case of rape, the cost of unconsented sex is very high. Third, one must evaluate what is being pursued in relation to the consequences of non-consent by one's partner. In the case of consent versus non-consent, this is the value to the man of having sex with this woman in this place at this time. However, the loss of sexual gratification in one instance does not preclude future sexual gratification. Following this logic, the risk of a failure to be gratified at one particular moment is minuscule when compared with the risk of engaging in unconsented sex with one's partner. Finally, there is the need to run the risk. Does Smith have to have sex with Jones when Jones does not consent? A man can always, with no substantial cost, obtain assurance that the sex he seeks is consensual. An explicit "yes" or "no" can be easily obtained. In conclusion, "a mistake as to the other's consent is unreasonable in as much as there is a risk of harming, possibly greatly harming, the other when little or nothing is gained for oneself by running this risk, and when the risk can always be avoided or greatly minimized at no significant cost to oneself by direct inquiry of the other" (Archard in Burgess-Jackson 1999).

The ancient argument still accepted in a few circles today, is that a verbal "no" does not always indicate non-consent. After all, women are taught that they should not make their sexual desires quite so evident. What if Jones says "no" to sex with Smith when she actually does want the sex? In response to this possibility, Jeffrey A. Gauthier writes that ". . . a woman's refusal of a sexual overture has not been taken as worthy of respect in itself, but rather as an invitation for a more aggressive approach" (Gauthier in Burgess-Jackson 1999). In context, this is a potentially dangerous stereotype of women and women's sexuality. When a woman says "no," the majority of woman truly do mean "no." Even if this were not the case, the potential harm of delayed sexual gratification pales in comparison to the potential harms of unconsented sex (Smith in Burgess-Jackson 1999).

As Gauthier stated above, and as many of the previously discussed court cases have said, many men simply do not take "no" to mean "no." In the presence of evidence to the contrary, men tend to use two cognitive methods to assume consent: either the woman is ambivalent, or her signs of protest are equivocal and therefore subject to interpretation in two different directions. If Smith believes Jones is ambivalent, he believes she is of two minds about sex with Smith. Part of her says "yes" while part of her says "no," and Smith judges that the greater part of her says "yes." Believing Jones' signs of protest are ambiguous may lead Smith to interpret them to mean either consent or dissent. As we have seen, many court cases seem to hinge on this fact. For example, a woman does not take the opportunity to flee from the accused rapist. This may be due either to being frozen in panicked fear or a willing complicity. The man interprets it to mean the latter. The notion of "equivocal conduct" places the onus back on the woman. This is similar to the way that lack of resistance is evidence of consent. This is to the advantage of alleged perpetrators of rape and to the detriment of victims. I think that this advantage accruing to accused rapists is above and beyond what defendants accused of other crimes enjoy. What gives Smith cause to believe Jones' conduct signifies consent (Archard in Burgess-Jackson 1999)?

According to Douglas Husak and George Thomas III, there are social conventions which a man may rely on to come to a mistaken belief in consent. These conventions allow consent to be assumed in the absence of any explicit declarations of consent or dissent. According to them, conventions regarding heterosexual sex are that women do not ask for sex when they want it, and that they give unexplicit consent to male courtship. Therefore, if a man relies on these social conventions to assume consent, his belief is reasonable. Thomas and Husak, however, overlook some crucial points. First, they do not acknowledge that men and women may attribute different meanings to the same behavior. Additionally, there is no good reason for women to modify their behavior in order to conform to male expectations (Davion in Burgess-Jackson 1999).

It is clear to this writer that the courts should eliminate this ambiguity and make clear in their decisions that when the victim says no, she means no. In cases of rape the court should not play psychologist and explore the various gradations of "no."

As Jean Hampton wrote, culpability is "the choice to supplant what one knows to be an authoritative rule with a different authority that sanctions the act one wishes to take" (1990). Not to accept "no" as no is a usurping of the woman's authority as the only legitimate source of her consent. When Jones protests and indicates lack of consent, Smith supplants the authoritative voice of the honestly protesting Jones with another who allows her protest to be read as equivocal. In *Morgan*, this substitution was literal. In that case, young men were invited by Morgan to have sex with his wife. He led them to believe that his wife enjoyed forced sex, and that any struggling or protests on her part should be understood as "play acting." In going through with this arrangement, the young men substituted the voice of Morgan's wife as the authoritative source of her wishes with the voice of Morgan. What he said became their guide as opposed to what she said. The fault of those young men lay in the fact that they gave priority to the testimony of someone other than the proper source of the relevant belief (Archard in Burgess-Jackson 1999).

In other cases which are not quite as literal as *Morgan*, the woman's authority is supplanted by a convention which is not of her making. These conventions, or stereotypes, should not apply. They violate individuality and individual authority. This makes the man as blind to the obvious source of a woman's consent as the young men in *Morgan* (Davion in Burgess-Jackson 1999). Therefore, men who follow stereotypes in order to infer consent rather than a woman's authoritative voice are just as culpable as the defendants in *Morgan*.

Some could argue that one does not voluntarily select one's beliefs. For example, one cannot "will" oneself to believe in Santa Claus or not believe in the Tooth Faerie. Following this argument to an absurd conclusion, since a person cannot believe other than he does, he cannot be held culpable for a belief. This writer believes that the appropriate counter-argument to that assertion is that the purpose of the law is to prevent significant harm to the innocent, and that such harm can result as much from carelessness as from deliberate acts. Therefore the law has a responsibility to enforce a duty of care, and encourage appropriate standards of behavior, including consensual sex (Aristotle 1994).

Further, when courts judge reasonableness in terms of consent, the judgment should not be in terms of that fictional character of legal literature; the "reasonable man." The "reasonable man" has been deemed to be the ordinary man in the street. He is objective and non-idiosyncratic. The law takes him to be the standard of what is generally believed to be "reasonable" (Walker 1980).

It is the opinion of this writer that the "reasonable man" standard is inapplicable in terms of rape. In many areas of sex the reasonable man has been misled. He has believed that feigned displays of female pleasure are genuine ones. He can also mistakenly and unreasonably believe that a woman has consented to sex with him. In fact, the law's "reasonable man" has indeed overridden the authoritative voice of a woman with the voice of another person (DPPv. Morgan), or with a stereotype (Ellis 1989). The "reasonable man" is a man, using a strictly masculine standard of "reasonableness" (Archard in Burgess-Jackson 1999).

I believe that the method proposed here is preferable. The man should be penalized if he undercuts the woman's authoritative voice, substituting it with other "voices" which, in his mind, allow him to have sex with her. Be these voices the voice of her husband or mere conventions which state that "no" does not necessarily mean no, they are all similarly unreasonable. The "reasonable man" can be taken in by them. I believe that my proposed standard is also superior to the utmost resistance standard, the corroboration requirement, and the present day interpretation of "forcible compulsion." I also believe that this will lessen the undue protection enjoyed by accused rapists.

At this point it could be asserted that trial proceedings in our society have traditionally been skewed in favor of the defendant. While I do believe in the principle of it being preferable to let ten guilty people go free than to punish one innocent person, I also opine that rape defendants envoy too great of an advantage. As we have seen, the deck has historically been vastly stacked against rape victims. A woman should not have to be found unconscious in a pool of blood in order to obtain a conviction. The proposed reforms would not weaken the constitutional protections of the accused. The accused would still have to be found guilty of overriding a woman's authoritative voice beyond a reasonable doubt. He would also have to be found guilty by the unanimous decision of a jury of his peers.

XI) *Responses*

I would now like to address some potential criticisms which could be raised against my arguments. First, it could be argued that I advocate treating rape as a "special" crime. After all, in all other trial settings the defendant is mostly shielded from questions concerning her or his past which could prejudice the jury against her or him. Likewise, witnesses can be interrogated about their past in order to damage their credibility as reliable witnesses. Why is rape any different? Why, in a rape trial, should these traditions of exposure and protection differ?

I believe that this is not a valid criticism because rape trials are quite unique. Like murder, rape is taken to be a crime against the state. Unlike murder, rape involves both a living victim and a living defendant. Since rape is in a strictly legal sense a crime against the state and not the victim, the victim can be called as a witness. Furthermore, as a witness, the victim can be grilled concerning her sexual past in order to cast doubt on her credibility. However, in a rape trial, the defense counsel is not just questioning a witness. He is questioning the victim of the crime herself, and the questioning of a rape prosecutrix is usually aggressive. On the grounds of humanity, a rape victim should be granted some protection when cross-questioned. I am not advocating that rape cases be treated differently; I couldn't even if I wanted to. They already are.

Secondly, one could offer a counterplan. At my thesis defense, it was suggested that "well-defined, objective side constraints might be useful." That is, objective factors could be brought out by the state in order to support conviction. The defense would then have to focus on these objective factors. The trouble with this is that the circumstances surrounding a rape are rarely well-defined. In cases of simple rape, one would be very hard pressed to find "well-defined, objective side constraints."

In fact, some of the objective factors proposed at my defense were "use of a weapon, that the rape was committed in the course of another crime, absence of any prior contact between accused and accuser." All of these indicate an instance of *aggravated* rape, rape perpetrated by a stranger. As previously stated, most rapes are not aggravated. A woman is much more likely to be raped by an acquaintance than she is by a stranger. It is also much more likely that a weapon will *not* be involved. A woman is much more likely to be a victim of a *simple* rape where these objective factors could not come into play. Furthermore, since my paper is primarily devoted to simple rapes, I consider this objection not pertinent to my thesis.

Finally, one could argue that the data I rely on is dated. For instance, one of my primary sources, Susan Estrich's *Real Rape* is copyrighted 1987. The current definition of rape and forcible compulsion, however, has not changed since then. It must still be proven, as it did back when Estrich was writing her book, that a rapist either used force or threatened to do so. If a rapist does not either force the woman or threaten to force her, the law does not see him as a rapist. Legally, he is a seducer.

Rape is a horrible crime with dramatic negative ramifications for the people who undergo it. It is traumatic, misunderstood, and underreported. Its history is vast and highly disturbing, and many misconceptions about it still exist today. However, a standard of reasonableness involving a duty of care has the potential to reduce the rate of this atrocious act. This duty of care would involve, quite simply, a man taking a woman's "no" to be a "no," be it verbal or physical, and give her credit for knowing her mind when she speaks it aloud. It is up to the courts and legislators to formulate this law.[2]

Notes

1 This statement is the basis, although not the actual wording, of the "cautionary instruction" given to jurors at rape trials, in addition to the warning that guilt must be proven beyond a reasonable doubt.

2 This is dedicated to all the courageous survivors of rape who have helped pave the way for more just rape legislation. I would like to thank Steve, Adam, Greg and Tom for their support, feedback, and many hours of arcane philosophical debate. Also, thanks to mom, dad, and of course Shell (*Hag! Queen!*).

Works Cited

Aristotle. *Nichomachean Ethics.*

Blackstone, Sir William. *Commentaries on the Laws of England.* London: Dawsons of Pall Mall, 1966.

Burgess-Jackson, Keith, ed. A Most Detestable Crime: *New Philosophical Essays on Rape.* New York: Oxford University Press, 1999.

Columbia Law Review. "Corroborating Charges of Rape." Vol. 67, 1967.

Ellis, Lee. *Theories of Rape: Inquiries into the Causes of Sexual Aggression.* New York: Hemisphere Publishing Corporation, 1989.

Estrich, Susan. *Real Rape.* Cambridge: Harvard University Press, 1987.

Estrich, Susan. *Sex and Power.* New York: Riverhead Books, 2000.

Finkelhor, David and Kersti Yllo. *License to Rape: Sexual Abuse of Wives.* New York: Holt, Rinehart and Winston, 1985.

Hale, Sir Matthew. *The History of the Pleas of the Crown.* London: Professional Books, 1971.

Hampton, Jean. "Mens Rea." *Social Philosophy and Policy*, 7 (1990): pp. 1-28.

L'Armand, Kathleen, and Albert Pepitone. "Judgments of Rape: A Study of Victim-Rapist Relationship and Victim Sexual History," *Personality and Psychology Bulletin*, 8 (March 1982).

Madigan, Lee and Nancy Gamble. *The Second Rape: Society's Continued Betrayal of the Victim.* New York: Lexington Books, 1991.

Model Penal Code and Commentaries (1980), sec. 213.6.

Penal Law, sec. 130.30, McKinney's Annotated Laws of New York.

Schulhofer, Stephen J. *Unwanted Sex: The Culture of Intimidation and the Failure of Law.* Cambridge: Harvard University Press, 1998.

Stanford Law Review. "The Resistance Standard in Rape Legislation." Vol. 18, February 1966.

Taslitz, Andrew E. *Rape and the Culture of the Courtroom.* New York: New York University Press, 1999.

Tomaselli, Sylvana and Roy Porter, eds. *Rape.* Oxford: Basil Blackwell, 1986.

U.S. Congress. House. Select Committe on Children, Youth, and Families. 1990. *Hearing on Victims of Rape*, June 28th.

Walker, David M. *The Oxford Companion to Law.* Oxford: Clarendon Press, 1980.

Yale Law Journal Company. "Forcible and Statutory Rape." *Yale Law Journal,* Vol. 62 (December 1952).

Bibliography of Court Cases

Alston, State v., 312 S.E.2d 470, (1984).

Bailey v. the Commonwealth, 82 Va. 107, (1886).

Biescar, People v., 58 Cal. App. 722, (1929).

Brown v. State, 127 Wis. 193, (1906).

Christian v. the Commonwealth, 64 Va. 954, (1873).

Connelly, State v., 57 Minn. 482, (1894).

Evans, People v., 379 N.Y.2d 912, (1975).

Hart v. the Commonwealth, 131 Va. 726, (1921).

Liberta, People v., 64 N.Y.2d 152, (1984).

Mlinarich, the Commonwealth v., 498 A.2d 395, (1985).

Morgan, Director of Public Prosecutions v., [1975] 2 W.L.R. 923 (H.L.).

Packineau v. United States, 202 F.2d 681 (1953).

Steward v. State, 145 So. 162, (1932).

Abstract

With the increase in economic globalization and a decrease in border controls, people have become more aware of human rights violations worldwide. To ensure economic success for all nations, there must be a list of human rights that applies universally to all individuals. Although the United Nations has enumerated such a list in the Universal Declaration of Human Rights (UDHR), it cannot properly protect all individuals because it only applies to nation-states. In order to guarantee proper protection of human rights, initiatives must start at the state level when people understand their basic rights and demand that the government provide for them.

EXAMINING THE RELATIONSHIP BETWEEN ECONOMIC GLOBALIZATION AND HUMAN RIGHTS

Rachel Baskin

Economic globalization has led to a decrease in nation's border controls. As a result it is easier to move goods and services across borders without regulations or restrictions. Furthermore, the labor market has become global, insofar as people are moving across countries' borders. The movement of goods, services and people has made us become more connected as a global society. This interconnectedness has brought human rights into a new light, making us concerned with human rights violations worldwide. A decrease in economic border controls has led to trading and production agreements with universal terms, such that the terms of trade are not being "imposed" on any party. However, the only universal principle in terms of social and political rights is the universal principle of national sovereignty, such that any interference is often looked upon as an imposition of "Western norms" or as imperialistic.

New political forces and technological changes have helped to change our conceptions of human rights, which evolve over time. While human rights evolve we must take care to ensure that the proper institutions are in place to ensure their proper protection. Currently, the United Nations (UN) fails to protect individuals' human rights. The UN protects its members, sovereign nations; therefore individuals who suffer from human rights violations often have difficulty finding remedies for such violations. The UN has no police power to ensure that each member state promotes the rights enumerated in the UN Charter, or in the Universal Declaration of Human Rights. Furthermore, in the Universal Declaration of Human Rights, the UN proposes a vast number of rights, enumerated in thirty articles, which all carry the same weight. Since human rights- rights granted to individuals by virtue of their being human beings- are of such great importance, a smaller list of the most basic rights should be enumerated and guaranteed by an institution that can ensure their proper protection more efficiently than the UN. As Amartya Sen points out, allowing such freedoms will enhance national economic success and development. A higher institution, where individuals have a voice, would ideally ensure the proper protection of rights, but would ultimately fail because it would require that nations give up some of their sovereignty. So, while sovereign nations surrender their control on economic terms, they are not willing to surrender total control in political and social terms in order to protect individuals' human rights.

I. Economic Globalization: The Increased Movement of Capital Flow

While border controls affecting capital flow continue to decrease, allowing further trade and economic growth, the same type of growth on political and social terms has not increased at the same rate. Border controls still exist, making intervention and change on political and social terms a difficult task. However, borders are becoming more and more porous. In the past, the international economy included only trade and investments between countries. National governments controlled the way their national economy was run- establishing laws controlling international and national trade and investment.

Due to an increase in technology and mobility, corporations have begun production in other nations, further changing the economy from an international economy to a global economy. In the global economy, corporations function in territories other than their own, producing goods and providing services. Tooze makes a distinction between the international economy and the global economy. He defines the international economy as the economic relations between and among nations, where the basic units are the national economies and the significant activities include trade, followed by investment. The definition of the global economy includes all the activities of the international economy, and is made up of firms and other entities operating transnationally over the whole globe. In the global economy, activities are geared toward the production of goods and services for a global market and much of a firm's activity takes place outside of the market within their own global structure. For example, an American firm that only used to trade goods with China in the international economy has now established factories in China so that they can produce goods in the global economy. (As I've read Tooze, I take him to mean that activities such as these, where firms provide and produce goods and services in foreign markets, is becoming a dominant practice in the global economy) (Tooze 1999: 220-221). Consequently, corporations become subject to the jurisdiction of the nations in which they do business.

As economic globalization has become a realization, national governments lose some of their influence regarding economic policy. Now, corporations account for a majority of the world's trade, and Kaplan notes that corporations are similar to "feudal domains that [have] evolved into nation-states" (Kaplan 1997: 71). National governments that could formerly regulate international and national trade are finding that the global economy is greatly unregulated. Corporations, interested in maximizing efficiency in order to maximize profit, are interested in doing business in areas that will have the lowest cost and fewest restrictions. If businesses do not like the regulations of one country, due the decrease of border controls, they are free to move their business to another country. As economics and politics are intertwined, in what Tooze refers to as the "International Political Economy," national governments, interested in economic growth brought by foreign corporations may have to change their policies in order to attract foreign corporations (Tooze 1999: 212).

The growth of the global economy has led to a decrease in the political control that nation-states maintain over their territories. Kaplan observes that although democratic governance continues at local, state and federal levels, its ability to affect our lives is limited (Kaplan 1997: 73). An international economy based on world markets and production has made it increasingly difficult to rely on an international political system based on sovereign nations, defined by their territorial borders (Tooze 1999: 214). Globalization has forced nation-states to open up to external regimes, weakening the scope of the national government. As Habermas explains, "markets drive out politics, nation-states lose their capacity to raise taxes and stimulate growth and the ability to secure the essential foundations of their own legitimacy" (Habermas 2001: 79). Furthermore, with the emergence of trading blocs, such as NAFTA, the European Community (EC), and ASEAN, national control of international trade becomes even more blurred.

Trading blocs are agreements formed by nations, generally within the same geographic region, in which trading restrictions are usually eliminated between the countries that enter into such agreements. Not all countries, however, can enter into these unregulated trading unions. As the most influential trading unions, NAFTA, the EC, and ASEAN have become more and more interdependent, countries excluded from these trading unions do not experience the same type of economic growth. A problem with these superpowers is that they permit few smaller countries to enter into the trading unions. Countries outside of the "Triad," as Tooze refers to the three trading unions, cannot catch up in terms of growth because they do not have access to the same resources as the most economically advanced countries.

Even if countries outside of the Triad have an abundance of resources, they do not have the technology to maximize their profit and enhance growth with these resources. For example, the International Monetary Fund (IMF) and World Bank (WB) have implemented policies that they encourage nations to adopt because such policies will increase their economic activity. These initiatives rarely help suffering nations, bur rather they help the corporations supporting such policies. For instance, in Africa, nations produce cash crops or add new technology, but cannot utilize the crops, or the technology in ways that benefit their national economies. Cocoa, for example must be sent o France to become chocolate, and the French economy gains more than the African producers of the cocoa. So, as the trading blocs of the Triad advance their own technology and grow economically, other countries are left behind and eventually they are not able to catch up and advance as much as the nations within the Triad. This leads to the polarization of the rich North and the poor South.

While the market and trading unions begin to gain control in international relations, the international community has become more aware of economic relations, and domestic policy comes under greater scrutiny. With the increase in trade and production outside of its own borders, corporations must adhere to the domestic policy of the country in which they do their business. The international community becomes concerned when corporations operate in nations with unfair or unjust domestic policies, which violate human rights.

For example, how should a business act if the country in which it has just opened a factory employs children to work forty hours a week? On the one hand, this new factory under the country's jurisdiction, will allow the foreign corporation to maximize efficiency and profit. On the other hand, the corporation does not think that children should be made to work, especially for such long hours. Should the corporation's home country impose trade sanctions to encourage this country to create child labor laws, or should it allow the corporation to manage its new factory? Trade sanctions against human rights violations are not always clearly or directly tied to the violation, therefore the legitimacy of the sanctions may appear questionable (Donnelly 1998: 153).

II. Business Control: The Global Compact

The United Nations has tried to implement social and political change through businesses to solve the aforementioned dilemma that businesses may face. It has created the Global Compact, which it asks businesses to join, hoping to affect change in the political and social spheres through the economic sphere. The UN recognizes the impact of economic globalization and the decrease in border controls. It wants corporations to partake in activities that promote UN goals included in the UN Charter and the Universal Declaration of Human Rights. Kofi Annan, Secretary-General of the UN, describes the Global Compact as a "proposal for world business leaders to help build social and environmental pillars required to sustain the new global economy and make globalization work for all the world's people" (*United Nations Global Compact*).

The Global Compact tries to use dialogue to identify good practices that lie within the established Nine Principles based on the Universal Declaration of Human Rights. The UN explains that firms should incorporate the Nine Principles because business has gone global and firms can influence other nations through their leadership. The UN has appealed to governments, civil society organizations, labor organizations and corporations to become advocates for the Global Compact. It hopes that participants will produce mission statements, annual reports, and newsletters in public venues in order to create a dialogue of what works and what does not work when trying to adhere to the Nine Principles. Corporations that join must participate in an annual dialogue to help improve rights violations throughout the world. The UN hopes that such postings and dialogue will promote the aims of global corporate citizenship and corporate social responsibility (*United Nations Global Compact*).

The Nine Principles it asks corporations to follow are broken down into three categories: human rights, labor and environment:

> **Human Rights**—World businesses should
> 1. support and protect international human rights in their sphere of influence; and
> 2. ensure that their own corporation is not complicit in any human rights abuses.
>
> **Labor**—World businesses should uphold
> 3. freedom of association and the right to collective bargaining;
> 4. the elimination of forced and compulsory labor;
> 5. the abolition of child labor; and
> 6. the elimination of discrimination in respect of employment and occupation.
>
> **Environment**—World businesses should
> 7. support a precautionary approach to environmental challenges;
> 8. undertake initiatives to promote greater environmental responsibility; and
> 9. encourage development and diffusion of environmentally friendly technologies (*United Nations Global Compact*).

Few corporations have joined the Global Compact and there is little incentive for corporations to join to affect change. Insofar as businesses are concerned with maximizing profit and efficiency, implementing costly policies that require them to be socially responsible will reduce their actual profits. Therefore, the only thing that businesses stand to gain from joining the Global Compact is a good public reputation.

Furthermore, if the businesses are under the jurisdiction of the nation-state in which they operate, they cannot change the nation-state's laws. Insofar as businesses strive for profit, but face conflicting moral issues, Brown asks, "is it worth risking a trading contract in order to make a point about a violation of human rights, or...should one overlook an obvious wrong in the interest of profit?" (Brown 1999: 471). The Global Compact asks businesses to reach positive answers to these questions, but economic theory tells them otherwise. As long as they are under the jurisdiction of a foreign nation, they must adhere to the rules of that nation and in order to maximize profit they must act within the law, regardless of what that law may be. It is not up to businesses to decide whether a law is just or not, nor to induce change, as that will not help increase profits.

Moreover, the Global Compact asks business to "support and protect international human rights in their sphere of influence," but it does not define the sphere of influence (*United Nations Global Compact*). Should corporations be responsible only for their workers, should they extend their responsibility to workers' families, or even to the whole population surrounding their factory? Even if corporations do improve working standards within a nation, it is the individual's responsibility to choose to work under such standards (Sen 2000: 288). Or, if the sphere of influence includes people who do not work in the corporations' factories, there is no way for the corporations to directly affect the surrounding individuals' lives.

Although the proposal for the Global Compact strives to create a global community, by encouraging businesses to consider human rights, labor and the environment, it is inefficient for corporations and will ultimately fail to convince big corporations, who could be the most influential, to join. In order for the Global Compact to be successful, change must be willed by the individuals within the nations, who, in turn, will cooperate with corporations to induce the change. Corporations cannot induce the change on their own while under the jurisdiction of another nation, because it could be seen as a type of intervention, which the UN Charter strictly prohibits. The UN Charter, which defines the make-up of the members of the United Nations, does not recognize businesses. As business has had greater impact on nation-states, affecting the global community, the UN now seeks to maintain peace through the Global Compact.

III. The United Nations: Its Inability to Protect Human Rights

The United Nations, formed after World War II, purported to enhance international relations and international law for all its member nations. It yearned to form a type of global community in which nation-states lived together peacefully. The UN Charter specifies the goals and the purposes of the international institution. Among its goals are: to respect the principle of equal rights and self determination of people; promote high standards of living and economic development; and promote universal respect for human rights and fundamental freedoms for all without distinction as to race, sex, language or religion (*United Nations Charter*). The Charter also defines the composition of the members of the United Nations. Members consist in sovereign nations, not in the people of the nation. According to Article 2 of the Charter, the UN is based on "the sovereign equality of all its Members" and denies all member nations the right to "intervene in matters that are essentially within the domestic jurisdiction of any state..." (*United Nations Charter*).

After establishing the UN Charter, the United Nations created the Universal Declaration of Human Rights (UDHR). The UDHR appeals to all people and all nations, asking them to agree to meet a common standard of rights, promoting universal respect and recognition for the enumerated rights. Some of the rights included within the UDHR are: the rights of everyone to be born free and equal in dignity and rights;

life, liberty, and security; freedom of thought and religion; freedom from discrimination; and the abolition of slavery, servitude and the slave trade (*United Nations Universal Declaration of Human Rights*). The UDHR, like the UN Charter, also applies only to sovereign states, and asks the nations to apply the principles to the people of their own nation, as well as to the territories under their jurisdiction. As with the UN Charter, intervention is prohibited.

The UN principles, which find the nation-state at the center of control, base their policies on the theory that each sovereign nation is responsible for the individuals within that nation. The basic principle that the UN seeks to uphold is the sovereignty of the states, which outweighs any principle of intervention. Typically human rights, seen as the state's control of its people, fell under nation-states' domestic jurisdiction. Individuals recognized as citizens under the law of specific territories expect that these territories provide them with basic rights. Sovereign nations are responsible for providing their citizens with basic needs such as food, shelter, education, healthcare and security. The state has the authority to provide individuals with these rights, making them legitimate through government implementation. Therefore the UN tries to encourage development of institutions to protect human rights at the regional level. While the UN tries to protect all indivudals' rights through this method, we can see how it fails democratically. Individuals do not have a say in the rights that the UN tries to protect. Individuals do not elect representatives to represent them in the UN, so they have no voice within the institution.

Recognizing member states as sovereign members, the UN also recognizes states' rights to rule within their jurisdiction and asserts that member states follow the principles established by the UN in good faith. There is no UN police to determine whether or not nation-states are upholding the principles they agreed to when they became members of the UN.

Since there is no police power, and individuals find it difficult to report human rights violations, the UN Charter as well as the Universal Declaration of Human Rights cannot protect the human rights of all individuals throughout the world by applying only to sovereign nations. Individuals cannot report human rights violations directly to UN committees to have them remedied. When individuals try to seek remedies through UN procedures, they must show that all domestic remedies have been exhausted and that violations were not sporadic. Once the UN agrees to help, the help comes in the form of cooperation with the government of the country where the alleged violation took place. Once again, with the absence of police power, there is no way to ensure that all human rights violations have been eradicated. Richard Falk attests that the

> absence of any real prospect of enforcement makes it feasible for some governments to ratify agreements that they cannot keep, while other governments that might observe them are deterred from becoming parties to conventions by theoretical possibility of enforcement (qtd. in Vincent 1986: 99).

Therefore, signatures on agreements do not ensure that they are properly carried out, and the lack of enforcement power devalues agreements, such that governments have little reason to sign. Ultimately, nation-states decide what policies to implement and how they should implement them. Standards that are established at the international level are not always carried out at the national level. This is indicative of an institutional inefficiency from which the UN suffers.

The only way in which the UN remotely provides help directly to individuals within sovereign nations is through recognized Non-Governmental Organizations (NGOs). The UN works with some NGOs who are responsible for reporting human rights violations to the UN and helping the country rectify violations. One problem with NGOs is that they function on the same premise as the Global Compact, relying on the power of publicity and persuasion. They feel that countries, like corporations, will care so much about their reputation outside of their country, that bad public opinion will cause them to change, eliminating human rights violations. As with corporations, countries do not find this a sufficient reason for change. Furthermore, NGOs lack legitimacy, such that the national government is still supreme. The UN cannot maintain the proper protection of human rights through NGOs nor through state governments with which it will not intervene.

The UN could be more successful at eradicating human rights violations if it established a court, similar to the International Court of Justice, through which individuals or nation-states could report human rights violations- in civil or criminal lawsuits. The court that the UN would have to establish would be different from the International Court of Justice in that individuals would be able to bring cases to the court. The statute of the International Court of Justice explains that only states may be parties in cases before the court. The problem with this though, is what to do if the court finds that a country violates human rights. Who is responsible? Once other nations intervene, they are imposing their own policies on a nation that may not be able to succeed by adopting such policies. If the court does not find the country guilty of violating human rights, then individuals who feel that the decision is wrong, have no way to appeal, and must continue to suffer from violations.

Another alternative is to adopt intervention methods through which member states agree to be tried in international courts if other nations find that they have committed human rights violations. This makes the notion of sovereign immunity obsolete. Member states would not sign such an agreement because they would feel that it violates the principle on which the UN accepts its legitimacy, that of state sovereignty.

IV. Universality of Human Rights: The List to be Protected

As we can see, the UN cannot protect human rights efficiently even though it has established the Universal Declaration of Human Rights, with which it expects member nations to comply. However, without any form of police power, such a long list, as the one enumerated, cannot be properly enforced. As human rights are so important that they should be granted to all individuals, perhaps the list enumerated by the UN should be shortened to include only a list of fundamental rights through which other rights or freedoms will arise. If we shorten the list of rights to be protected to include only the basic, fundamental rights, then nation-states can choose how to implement policies to ensure their proper protection. Nation-states could provide for these fundamental rights in ways that will be most beneficial to their societies. Basic human rights-rights that arise by virtue of being human beings, protect the dignity of all humans against threats that may fundamentally violate these rights. Peter Jones defends a notion of universal human rights insofar as

> they are intrinsic to the Law of Peoples and have a political (moral) effect whether or not they are supported locally. That is, their political (moral) force extends to all societies, and they are binding on all peoples and societies, including outlaw states (qtd. in Rawls: 2001: 80-81).

The rights approved by the UDHR can be explained by breaking them down into, as Brown calls them, First, Second and Third Generation rights. First Generation rights are broad political rights, associated with liberal "Western" policies such as freedom of speech, religion, and assembly. Second Generation rights include economic and social issues, such as the right to an adequate standard of living and the right to an education. Third Generation rights refer to the rights of peoples, such as the right to preserve one's culture (Brown 1999: 470). First Generation Rights are broader, in a universal sense, in that they can be held against everyone else. Second Generation rights are enjoyed by everyone, but they impose duties on governments.

The UN should not rely on such a broad list of human rights to be applied universally. Some of the rights enumerated in the UDHR conflict with domestic law in some nations, and consequently with the underlying principle of the UN that members should maintain control over their national law. Rather than signing the Universal Declaration of Human Rights, nations such as South Africa and Saudi Arabia abstained. South Africa objected to the Declaration at the time of signing, because it had implemented Apartheid, and did not agree with the provision of Article 1, "that all are born free and equal in dignity and rights." Furthermore, according to Brown, South Africa rejected the Declaration because violated Article 2, section 7 of the Charter, which allows nations to maintain control over domestic matters (Brown 1999: 476). Saudi Arabia, objected, appealing to Third Generation rights, and denied that the UDHR was at all universal. As Brown notes, Saudi Arabia claimed that their country was different from others, specifically because the "the Saudi Ruler is Custodian of the Holy Places of the One True Religion," so different rules should apply to Saudi Arabia (Brown 1999: 476).

The most agreed upon principle that the UN recognizes is the universal understanding of state sovereignty. Therefore it is difficult to establish a list of human rights that is universally accepted in all nations. Insofar as we value our national sovereignty and the need for human rights laws, Chris Brown points out that "the things that distinguish us from one another are as important as the things that unite us, [e.g. our common humanity]" (Brown 1999: 479). The enumerated rights in the UDHR do not rely on a world consensus of the rights that should be protected.

This elucidates the problem of nation-states signing treaties for human rights without actually implementing sufficient policies. By including such a broad notion of all the rights to be protected, the UN cannot focus on those rights that are the most important and fundamental. Since human rights are so important, the list should be narrowed in order for the UN, or another international institution to provide for their proper protection. Chris Brown suggests that since there is no common language through which we can discuss human rights universally, that we discuss human wrongs. Explaining Michael Walzer, Brown offers that

> there may be no thick moral code that is universally acceptable, to which all local codes conform, but there may be a thin code which at least can be used to de-legitimize some actions (qtd. in Brown 1999: 481).

Accordingly, there can be definite human wrongs. Actions that are not worthy of respect would fall into the category of human wrongs. For example, genocide cannot be worthy of respect in any local community and must be condemned as a human wrong.

Instead of applying the list established by the UN, a new refined list of human rights should be established, focusing on the minimal protections necessary. The list should also be agreed on by all nations, such that the provisions do not conflict with national policy. Freedoms will subsequently arise if the minimal list is properly enumerated and adhered to. Human rights would be properly protected. Such a list could be established by appealing to Isiaih Berlin's concept of negative and positive liberties. In order to protect human rights, we have to find the proper balance between these two concepts. Minimal protections must be afforded through negative liberties and positive liberties will then follow.

Berlin defines negative liberties as those freedoms with which no one has a right to interfere. He defends this principle by stating that there exists a sphere of non-interference around individuals such that within the sphere individuals can act as they wish, avoiding interference by other persons. Berlin questions the extent to which individuals live in such a sphere, and what rights are afforded to citizens when they enter the sphere of non-interference. An example of a negative liberty would be the First Amendment to the United States' Constitution, which states, in part, that "Congress shall make no law… abridging the freedom of speech...." Americans have commonly coined this right the freedom of speech, which may imply that it is a positive liberty, however it a negative liberty in the sense that Congress cannot interfere with your right to speak freely.

Positive liberties, on the other hand, concern an individual's freedom to do and accomplish things. Berlin explains that positive liberties allow the individual to become his own master, such that he is responsible for all his own actions. While negative liberties can be thought of as freedom from interference, positive liberties lead to the notion of the freedom to- the freedom to act, as an individual, as his own master.

While extreme implementation of negative liberties may lead to a society where no one enjoys the freedom to choose for himself, it is important that we secure negative liberties. If we fail to preserve negative liberties, we will be unable to pursue positive liberties should we desire. Governments' role is to protect the negative liberties of its citizens. Berlin argues that rights, not power are absolute. Insofar as positive liberties dictate who has the power and the form of power can change from democracy to tyranny, all those in power are required to respect individual's rights via negative liberties.

By appealing to Berlin's concept of negative liberties, we can shorten the UN's Universal Declaration of Human Rights to include only those rights that protect negative liberties. We must ensure that all individuals have a sphere of non-interference, so that no matter what form of government they live under, their negative liberties will always be protected. Furthermore, it will be easier to protect a shorter list of rights in the form of negative liberties. Once a sphere of non-interference is established, positive liberties will emerge. If the UN focused on protecting negative liberties such as all people are born free and equal, such that no one could interfere with equality of people, then it would not have to focus on ideas such as equality in familial relations because that would follow from the negative liberty.

A criticism of narrowing the list would state that we could not protect rights properly by narrowing down the list of human right as much as Berlin's theory would require. Rather, we would have to provide for First and Second Generation rights. Without a government or institution in place that protects Second Generation rights, there cannot be protection of the basic rights. For example, if a government does not provide basic education for its citizens, which is a Second Generation right because it is a social right, then the citizens will not be aware of their rights, nor will they be able to demand their protection. They will not be able to employ their rights for basic rights such as voting. Therefore, basic rights emerge from a combination of First and Second Generation rights. Without the incorporation of Second Generation rights, basic rights cannot be realized.

Amartya Sen offers an alternative to Berlin's theory. Sen argues that by increasing human capabilities we can increase individual freedoms. Sen lists freedoms in terms of economic, social and political rights. It is the role of governments to protect these freedoms. Governments have incentive to promote these freedoms, Sen argues, because they will lead to development and economic growth. More specifically, Sen identifies the essential freedoms as political freedoms, economic facilities, social opportunities, transparency guarantees, and protective security (Sen 2000: 38). Ensuring these freedoms helps contribute to the development and the overall capabilities of people. Sen explains each of these instrumental freedoms and how they contribute to human capabilities.

Political freedoms are like positive liberties in that they concern individuals' opportunities to decide by whom they should be ruled and with what principles. Furthermore, they relate to First Generation rights because they include such freedoms as the freedom of press and assembly. Sen warns that they are democratic ideals only in the broadest sense. Economic facilities relate to Second Generation rights insofar as they give individuals economic freedom. Economic entitlements are to rely strictly on market mechanisms such that each individual can use his economic resources for the purposes of consumption, production, or exchange. Social opportunities also relate to Second Generation rights because they are concerned with education and healthcare. Insofar as Second Generation rights are concerned with a good standard of living, social opportunities seek to provide a standard of living which enhances all individuals' freedoms. By improving social opportunities, other freedoms will be enhanced. For example, an educated person will increase his or her opportunity for success in both the political and economic arenas. Transparency guarantees refer to the trust that governments must establish with their people. In order for people to succeed in their environment they must trust their government. This prevents things such as corruption and financial irresponsibility. Finally, individuals must be afforded some form of protective security. Governments should support institutions that promote security, as a safety net for individuals within the society. Institutions should provide some form of unemployment benefits, or emergency public employment in order to bring nations out of the shock induced by disaster (e.g. famines) (Sen 2000: 38-40).

Sen observes that by providing these fundamental freedoms, a basic set of human rights will emerge. For example, protecting political freedoms will lead to a greater amount of equality. Through equality, we can eradicate problems in education, infant mortality and female deaths during childbirth. Furthermore, rights such as equality in marriage will no longer need to be specified because this right would emerge from the right of equality.

Insofar as human rights are to be protected because they maintain human dignity, Sen claims that enhancing capabilities through these fundamental freedoms will give individuals lives that they have reason to value. The list offered by Sen is also shorter than the Universal Declaration of Human Rights. Furthermore, it explains to governments how to protect individuals' rights better than the UDHR. Although it does not prescribe specific formulas for protecting human rights, it offers suggestions to governments on how to increase human capabilities. Sen's rights combine Berlin's concept of negative and positive liberties in order to achieve freedom, which will further development.

While there may be no agreed upon universal human rights that can be enumerated in a list as the UN desires, protection of human rights cannot be ignored. Human rights are so important that making a long list, as the UN does, will not provide for their protection. Human rights should be protected by creating a minimal list through Berlin's notion of negative liberties. Every individual should have his own sphere of non-interference with which no government can interfere. Governments, on the other hand, should implement policies that protect individuals' spheres of non-interference and enhance their capabilities, as prescribed by Sen. Once negative liberties are properly protected greater protection for human rights will emerge. Governments should be enthusiastic about such policies insofar as they will enhance economic development and growth. The UN, as a supranational institution where sovereign nations are members, cannot achieve such a goal.

Human rights cannot be guaranteed by an institution where the members include nation-states, and not the individuals within the state. In order for rights to be guaranteed, there has to be a public forum in which individuals can express themselves and demand protection for their rights. Through public discussion, where all individuals must be free to participate, a list of human rights will emerge.

V. Maintaining Multiculturalism: Universal Human Rights through Economic Incentive

A problem that we face by appealing to Berlin and Sen's notions of rights is that focusing on such rights may be looked upon as imposition of "Western" norms in other societies. Although the UN recognizes, the right to a cultural identity in its Universal Declaration of Human Rights, based on Berlin's theory of negative liberties and the creation of a minimal list of human rights, cultural identity would not be included in a list of basic protections. While it may not be necessary to provide special provisions for the protection of cultural rights, such rights must be respected; they have their own intrinsic value within the culture.

The doctrine of cultural relativism, as defined by R.J. Vincent, contains three provisions regarding the respect and legitimacy of cultural rights. First, rules about morality vary from place to place. Second, the way to understand variety is to place it in its cultural context. Lastly, moral claims derive from their cultural context, which is the source of their validity (Vincent 1986: 37). Insofar as there is movement across national borders, making political communities more heterogeneous in cultural terms, Donnelly suggests that such cultural variability requires significant allowance for cross-cultural variation in human rights (Donnelly 1989: 112). Rather than enumerating a list of universal rights, we should recognize that rights vary cross-culturally. Therefore, we should be sure to protect cultural rights to ensure that all rights are protected within their cultural context. Traditional cultures, like political communities, provide members with a place in society and a certain amount of dignity and protection (Donnelly 1989: 120). Insofar as we protect human rights to ensure that all humans live dignified lives; we should not dismiss the argument to protect cultural rights because cultural communities provide a certain amount of dignity to their members.

Some arguments for the protection of cultural rights claim that trying to apply a universal doctrine of human rights is an imperialistic act. If we agree to respect other cultures, we should agree to permit them to accept cultural values as they see just. We should treat human rights as rights that most societies recognize. We should define them in terms of the values in their particular culture (Vincent 1986: 48). By judging cultures from the outside, we impose our outside views, and cannot understand the practice within its natural context. In order to understand the practice completely, we must accept it as it relates to the community. We must recognize that each culture has a pattern of life that is of equal validity to all others. Vincent further explains the doctrine of cultural relativism by stating that we cannot rank cultures in terms of equal or unequal. We can only observe the values that are derived in the culture. We cannot judge the values from an external standpoint. He continues by criticizing cultural relativity, stating that people who accept the doctrine allow the predominant opinion of any locality to prevail whether or not they have good reasons to support it. (Vincent 1986: 54). When other communities' values do not coincide with our "Western" notion of rights, we should refrain from intruding on the group's sphere of non-interference.

Other arguments contest that cultures within a political society should be afforded special protections to ensure that they do not lose their cultural identity. For example, immigrants who wish to assimilate also hope that assimilation will not require them to give up their cultural values. Charles Taylor introduces a dichotomy involving the protection of cultural rights. On the one hand, rights should include the protection of the basic rights of individuals as humans. On the other hand, rights should acknowledge the particular needs of individual members of specific cultural groups (Gutman 1994: 8). He urges governments to permit the special treatment of different cultures so they can thrive. Taylor questions whether or not liberal ideals properly protect cultural rights. Rights are formed with the notion that they should protect individuals' dignity. Insofar as this is true, as long as we mutually respect all cultures, we need no special provisions to protect cultural rights. Vincent notes however, that human rights awareness is not a challenge to communities' values or to state sovereignty, but rather something that adds to their legitimacy (Vincent 1986: 151).

When nations or cultures face turmoil, the protection of cultural values does not carry the same weight as when there is peace. In times of strife, governments must allow individuals to make choices to help them overcome disasters such as famines. In such cases, individuals must be granted the power to choose. Sen points out the conflicts that arise from the choice between

> 1) the basic value that people must be allowed to decide freely what traditions they wish or not wish to follow; and
> 2) the insistence that established traditions be followed (no matter what), or, alternatively, people must obey decisions by religious or secular authorities who enforce traditions- real or imagined (Sen 2000: 31-32).

He concludes that governments should ultimately provide all citizens with social, political and economic freedoms, as such freedoms lead to greater economic development and success. In response to arguments such as those of Lee Kuan Yew, former prime minister of Singapore, that assert that social and political freedoms hinder economic freedom and development, Sen argues that there is little empirical evidence to show that authoritarian regimes actually help economic growth (Sen 2000: 15). Furthermore, there is no evidence to suggest that authoritarian regimes that suppress rights have greater economic success than democratic regimes that grant civil rights and liberties. In fact, in democratic regimes where people can exercise their rights, people put pressure on their governments to adopt policies that will advance economic growth and development. Insofar as this is true, political rights can make a real difference (Sen 2000: 150-151).

Some Asian and African societies argue that such political rights conflict with their values that strongly support community values over "Western" norms. Human rights, in this view are purely Western values, and nations in the east do not want to embrace such a notion of rights. However, Habermas points out that Eastern societies have the same economic goals as the West; they want their economies to thrive. Habermas explains, what he calls, the "Asiatic values" dilemma of human rights, consisting of three problems.

In the first instance, human rights question the principle of rights over duties. Asiatic societies appeal to duties to a higher individual, or body, rather than to rights. For example, Habermas explains that ancient Asian and African cultures yield priority to a community over the individual and do not recognize a sharp distinction between law and ethics. In the second case, such values appeal to a particular "'hierarchy'" of human rights. Dictators of developing countries appeal to the priority of social commitments to the community to try to justify their violations against basic human rights of which they are accused. Such dictators claim that freedoms such as legal equity are not so relevant for the prospect of better living conditions. Lastly, Habermas explains that those with Asiatic values find that there are negative effects on the social order within the community when rights are granted to individuals (Habermas 2001: 123-125). While this is a simple depiction of the divide between the East and West, it can still help us see how protecting human rights, even in societies that do not appeal to any notion of rights, will be beneficial to their country.

Although Eastern values appeal to communitarian philosophy, the Western notion of rights will lead these societies to be economically successful like their counterparts in the west. By accepting economic modernization, Eastern nations can adopt the notion of individual human rights in order to attain economic success in its greatest capacity. In order to help increase economic success, Sen suggests that countries grant individuals certain freedoms. By increasing individuals' freedoms, economic growth and development will follow. He denies that he is rejecting the impact and value of different cultures by stating his

> belief in the ability of different people from different cultures to share many common values and to agree on some common commitments. [And that] the overriding value of freedom... [displays a] feature of strong universalist presumption (Sen 2000: 244).

He notes that Western norms are not required as long as the acting government provides its citizens with freedoms.

Coercion and suppression of rights do not help nations advance economically, as some advocates of Eastern values argue. For example, nations which impose restrictions on child bearing find that they have more trouble reducing their population than other nations that provide their citizens with the freedom to choose (Sen 2000: 222). For example, Sen notes that the coercion employed by China's government, by the one child policy has not been as successful in reducing the population as methods used in other countries. Coercion of this type has not been used in places such as Tamil Nadu or Kerala, yet both places have achieved much faster declines in fertility than China has (Sen 2000: 222).

Moreover, Sen argues that nations that deny equal opportunities based on cultural standards cannot succeed as much as those nations which grant opportunities to women. He says that

> some variables relating to women's agency...often play a much more important role in promoting social well-being...than variables relating to the general level of opulence in the society (Sen 2000: 198).

By granting individuals with freedoms, that may be contrary to communal values, Sen argues that countries will achieve more economic success than by relying on ideals that will not grant individuals such freedoms. Sen's theory can be applied to all individuals in all nations and to the newly formed global community that has been formed as a result in mobility in terms of immigration flow.

VI. Immigration: Formation of a Social Solidarity to Protect Human Rights

Due to an increase in the international labor market there are more incentives for people to leave their counties, and seek economic success in other ones. As border controls have weakened concerning economic movement, seeking labor in other countries becomes a feasible option for individuals. The UN recognizes the right to leave as one of our basic human rights. Although the UN remains controlling as a supranational institution recognizing the right to leave, it cannot order countries to accept policies concerning a similar right to enter. As Weiner points out, "the right to emigrate is understood as a basic right, while the right to immigrate is still regarded as a matter of individual state policy" (qtd. in Pensky 2002: 25). Instead of welcoming immigrants, countries often adopt policies limiting immigration flow. This perpetuates the problem of protecting human rights insofar as governments provide protection for members of a legal community to which immigrants do not belong.

Governments often adopt a picture of the needy immigrant who enters a country seeking benefits, therefore depriving members of the legal community of their deserved benefits. Immigrants are perceived as the poor and helpless of one country, because of negative consequences. Pensky offers that once we begin to accept negative consequences, such as poverty, as problems that lead to migration, we begin to see migration as a problem (Pensky 2002: 5). Rather than adopting this view, we should accept that immigrants include skilled laborers who seek to join another political community. The classical model of immigration offers that humans pledge their honor to their new commonwealth such that they adopt the laws of the land and wish to partake in political activities (Pensky 2002: 12). Immigrants seek to assimilate into new communities and agree to concede to the same obligations as citizens, while maintaining their cultural identities.

Although the same laws obligate immigrants and citizens alike, immigrants are not afforded protections in the same capacity as citizens. The question then arises, as to what rights should be afforded to immigrants, since they are not citizens of their new country. Should their new nation accept them as citizens in the liberal sense or in the communitarian sense? Pensky explains that citizenship in the liberal sense would require a set of legal protections ensuring a "relatively fair playing field where rational agents can genially compete." In the communitarian sense, citizenship is seen as composing a valuable resource for "collective identity, common virtues, and shared goals that provide the necessary context within which the liberal ideals of freedom and equality can be meaningfully practiced" (Pensky 2002: 31-32).

While immigrants are citizens of a world community with a growing economy, there are no universal protections guaranteed to them through this virtue. Human migration leads us to recognize the importance of a post-national form of social solidarity that immigrants can appeal to with the increase in migration due to a search for economic success (Pensky 2002: 9). The right to enter, and the rights afforded to immigrants can no longer be regulated in a purely domestic regime. There must be a post-national institution helping nation-states implement immigration laws to meet the needs of a globalized social community among immigrants and citizens. We need to build on this social solidarity and create immigration laws, concerning the right to enter and subsequent rights, through a supranational institution. Domestic regulations that cannot keep up with the increase in economic globalization can no longer control the increased immigration that arises as a result of the globalized economy.

VII. Policy Proposal: Organization for World Society

In order to see how we can better protect individuals' freedoms, due to the expanding market structure, which I've shown has led to our interconnectedness, I would like to suggest a utopian policy. I think that my policy would remedy the problems of the UN. It will be more efficient because there will some type of police power and it will be democratically legitimate insofar as individuals will be represented.

Since individuals partake in a global community in the economic sense, but not in the political or social sense, they need to unite to form a global community, an Organization for a World Society (OWS). Insofar as movement across borders has become more common, individuals must form a sort of civic solidarity, regardless of the borders that surround them. Individuals must be provided with a certain sphere of non-interference, such that they could abide by the laws that control their nation, if they so choose. At the same time they can also seek relief from a supranational institution concerned with the treatment of individuals in nation-states, regardless of the method the state adopts to remedy the violation. The institution must be assured that a nation that signs a treaty will carryout its provisions. It must provide protection for the individual. In order to provide proper protection, the institution would have to be democratic in nature such that all individuals had a voice. Individuals need to have a public sphere in which they can voice their concerns regarding possible human rights violations. People would be united through decisions that grant each other the necessary rights in order to be a legitimate society (Habermas 2001: 63).

The OWS will be a democratic institution through which representatives are elected in each nation-state by all individuals. The OWS will determine how many representatives each nation will have. Once individuals have elected representatives, the OWS representatives will elect members to become executive officials within the institution.

Once individuals within the Organization for World Society agree upon the standards of rights to be protected, based on the proper balance between Berlin's theory of positive and negative liberties, and Sen's capabilities hypothesis, they could agree on intervention policies and police power. Some may object, for example, by asking what sort of equality the OWS will insist upon- the distribution of resources, or equality of opportunity? By appealing to Berlin and Sen, it is not necessary to define what type of equality the OWS will insist upon. As long as nations' conception of equality meets the OWS's minimal standards of equality, then the OWS will not find any reason to intervene. Each nation-state can apply the concept of equality as they see fits their country.

Other critics may dispute shortening the list of rights that the OWS will protect by claiming that I am taking rights away from individuals, rather than granting them with more freedoms. However, if we appeal to Sen's capabilities hypothesis, we see that if we give individuals enough freedom or ability, they will be able to gain more. If the government affords them with their basic liberties, they will be able to increase their abilities, and attain more freedoms. For example, Sen points out that the deprivation for particular groups in very rich counties can be comparable to deprivation in third world countries. He examines the relationship between mortality and income and finds that African Americans have a considerably lower income than the white population in America, but are extremely rich in comparison to people in places such as Kerala and China. However, African Americans have a shorter life expectancy than individuals in both these places. Sen explains that

> it is not only the case that America blacks suffer from *relative* deprivation in terms of income per head vis-à-vis American whites, they are also *absolutely* more deprived than the low-income Indians in Kerala...and the Chinese...in terms of living to ripe old ages (Sen 2000: 21-22).

This demonstrates that individuals may have more freedoms comparatively, but are absolutely more deprived. More freedoms does not necessarily mean you are better off, as this study by Sen suggests. Shortening the list of protected rights not mean that people will have fewer rights; rather, they will be able to gain more freedoms from the basic list of rights that the OWS plans to guarantee to every individual in every nation.

The OWS would consequently be more inclusive than the UN, including individuals as well as groups, and extending the same rights universally. Individuals would be able to voice their concerns directly to the OWS. The OWS could then assist them through intervention insofar as it would help advance its goals. Sen writes, addressing why individuals as a global community should be concerned with human rights.

> [that although] no individual has direct reason to be concerned with justice and ethics, these considerations may be instrumentally important for economic success, and may, through that advantage, survive better than their rivals, in social rules of behavior (Sen 2000: 272-273).

Nation-states have lost their sovereignty in terms of regulating trade in the globalized economy. National governments' policies have little effect on the globalized market. Policies often restrict trade and harm the economy more than they help advance the countries' economic concerns. Therefore, as Sen argues, national governments should be concerned with granting individuals within their society with freedoms to ensure economic success in the globalized economy. Immigration would be among these freedoms, and as we've seen, immigration can no longer be regulated successfully at the national level. So the OWS would be legitimate insofar as it provides protections necessary to keep up with the globalized economy, that national governments cannot provide for their own citizens. The OWS can provide protection for human rights insofar as all nations want their economy to thrive and their countries to become more developed.

In the OWS, individuals will be concerned with the treatment of all humans, but will focus their energies to ensure the proper treatment of individuals within their nation-state. Therefore, the OWS can help individuals pressure their governments to ensure that their rights are not violated. Each individual within the OWS has the common goal of economic success and development, so they will want individuals to reap from such benefits. The OWS will have to create laws to constrain states that commit human rights violations. Steps toward intervention must be utilized and representatives should intervene with "outlaw states" by providing assistance. Plans of assistance would appeal to government officials who seek economic growth, and also to individuals within the nations who will gain the freedoms associated with economic growth.

John Rawls, in *The Law of Peoples* discusses a utopian society- the Society of Peoples that will provide assistance to outlaw states and burden states- those nations that do not comply with reasonable Law of Peoples and societies that deal with unfavorable conditions that prevent them from becoming members of the Society of Peoples, respectively. Once the Society of Peoples provides enough assistance to these outlaw and burdened states, the states will eventually become members of the Society of Peoples and the members of the society would have no reason to remain in the states. The OWS would have to work in a similar fashion.

In order to achieve sovereignty, the OWS has to be recognized by nation-states that accept their policies and methods of intervention. Nation-states will be willing to accept such intervention insofar as the policies implemented by OWS representatives ensure economic development and success. The OWS, as representatives of the people in the nation will implement policies that enhance their freedoms, and increase their sphere of non-interference so that they can also benefit from the economic success and development of their country. Furthermore, nation-states will allow the OWS to intervene as long as the OWS agrees to leave the nation-state once human rights violations have been eradicated according to their policies.

At the practical level, a society similar to the OWS has emerged. The European Union (EU) is a supranational institution, which states in Europe have given up some of their sovereignty to join. The EU was formed to unify European nations, and is similar to the UN in that its members exist as nation-states. The EU has created the European Court of Human Rights to address human rights violations that may occur within member nations. The Court has made nation-states more accountable for human rights violations that may occur within national borders. The EU provides an example of how a supranational institution, such as the OWS, would work at the international level. However the EU is not as inclusive as the OWS would be because it only includes certain member states, of Europe.

Such a society, like the OWS, would not be able to exist or thrive because states will still declare sovereignty. Rulers will not give up their rule or change it at such a great level as the OWS requires. Nor will rulers consent to the policies of the OWS if they are not convinced that such policies will increase the success of their economy. Appealing strictly to human rights violations will not convince governments to change their policies, because violations can be in the interest of the businesses that enhance national economies while committing human rights violations.

VIII. Need to Start at the State Level: "Grassroots" Movement

Since intervention cannot be justified through the United Nations, nor can change come about when an outside force imposes it; change must start at the bottom. In the case of nation-states, change cannot be imposed through supranational organizations. The UN cannot intervene, nor will individuals be able to participate in a world society to induce change. National governments will not surrender their sovereignty or power in order for a supranational institution to intervene, regardless of its effects on the national economy.

In order to properly protect human rights, individuals within nations must demand their protection within that nation-state. Vincent suggests that "change may require a shift in the pattern of political power...that can take place only with local commitment, not with outside imposition" (Vincent 1986: 146). As we have seen, outside imposition fails through UN initiatives. In addition sovereign states will not permit individuals to join together to form a supranational institution, like the OWS, committed to the protection of individual rights. Therefore, initiatives must start at the state level. Just as protecting a long list of human rights will fail because it causes institutions to focus on too many rights at once, enforcing policies through a supranational institution will fail on the same accord.

Once individuals are granted with their basic rights, they should focus on attaining those rights for all individuals within the nation. Although leaving the nation is an attractive option, insofar as individuals with knowledge can achieve more economic success, they should stay to help their country, rather than abandon it. Helping one's country can lead that country to economic success and development in the long run. The educated and privileged should stay to educate people so that all individuals within the nations realize that they have rights which should be afforded to them by their government. The people in individual sovereign nations must will the proper protection of human rights. Individuals in nation-states, once educated, must join together to demand that their governments implement effective social programs to protect human rights in ways that they see just.

IX. Conclusion

Although economic globalization has led to a decrease in border controls, sovereign nations still maintain sole control in political and social terms. Economic openness can only ensure a decrease in trade regulations, not an increase in the protection of human rights. Even with the decrease in trade regulations, nations are subject to unfair policies due to discrepancies in their economic strength and stability. Through economic success, though, such nations could increase in terms of development so that they would be able to compete internationally in the globalized economy.

The UN does not provide initiatives to help economies increase in a way that would advance human rights. Rather, it enumerates a long list of human rights, in thirty articles, which it cannot ensure is protected. The UN has no enforcement power, and relies on a strict policy of state sovereignty and non-intervention. By securing such a policy, the UN will never be able to secure the proper protection of human rights for all individuals.

Instead, a smaller list of human rights must be enumerated to include basic rights based on Berlin's theory of negative liberties. By adopting such a list, Berlin would argue that positive liberties, such as the freedoms enumerated by Sen, would emerge. Sen argues that if governments provide such freedoms to individuals, economic success and development will follow. Through such a system, governments will have to give individuals a voice so that their concerns may be heard. Individuals must be provided with a public sphere through which they can express their concerns with rights violations. Such a public sphere, however, cannot occur at the supranational level.

The role state sovereignty plays in our current international community is so big that nation-states would not be willing to give up their sovereignty and permit individuals to enter a public sphere at the international level, even if such an institution would help their economic structure. The only way to ensure the proper protection of human rights is for individuals in sovereign nations to demand that their government provide it. The educated people in nations must remain to teach the uneducated of the rights that they deserve, and must encourage them to demand such rights from their government. By appealing to state sovereignty through this route, individuals will have a say in what rights their governments should protect. Only then will human rights be protected in their greatest capacity. [1]

Notes

[1] Thank you so much to Max Pensky for being a great advisor and putting up with me, Steve Scalet for the Honor's Conference and working to get this published, Anna Feigenbaum for editing and support, and Elena Tenenbaum for being like a mom and supporting us.

Works Cited

Appiah, K. Anthony. "Identity, Authenticity, Survival: Multicultural Societies and Social Reproduction." *Multiculturalism: Examining the Politics of Recognition*. Ed. Amy Gutmann. Princeton, New Jersey: Princeton University Press, 1994. 149-163.

Bilder, Richard B. "An Overview of International Human Rights Law." *Guide to International Human Rights Practice*. 2nd ed. Ed. Hannum Hurst. Philadelphia, Pennsylvania: University of Pennsylvania Press, 1992. 3-18.

Berlin, Isiah. "Two Concepts of Liberty." *Four Essays on Liberty*. Oxford, England: Oxford University Press, 1969. 118-172.

Brown, Chris. "Human Rights." *The Globalization of World Politics: An Introduction to International Relations*. Ed. John Baylis and Steve Smith. Oxford, England: Oxford University Press, 1999. 469- 482.

Donnelly, Jack. *International Human Rights*. 2nd ed. Boulder, Colorado: Westview Press, 1998.

Donnelly, Jack. *Universal Human Rights in Theory and Practice*. Ithaca, New York: Cornell University Press, 1989.

Gutmann, Amy. "Introduction." *Multiculturalism: Examining the Politics of Recognition*. Ed. Amy Gutmann. Princeton, New Jersey: Princeton University Press, 1994. 3-24.

Habermas, Jurgen. "The Postnational Constellation and the Future of Democracy." *The Postnational Constellation*. Translated by Max Pensky. Cambridge, Massachusetts: The MIT Press, 2001. 58-112.

Habermas, Jurgen. "Remarks on Legitimation through Human Rights." *The Postnational Constellation*. Translated by Max Pensky. Cambridge, Massachusetts: The MIT Press, 2001. 113-129.

Habermas, Jurgen. "Struggles for Recognition." *Multiculturalism: Examining the Politics of Recognition*. Translated by Shierry

Weber Nicholsen. Ed. Amy Gutmann. Princeton, New Jersey: Princeton University Press, 1994. 107- 148.

Kaplan, Robert D. "Was Democracy Just a Moment?" *The Atlantic Monthly*. December 1997: 55-80.

Nye, Joseph S. *Understanding International Conflicts: An Introduction to Theory and History*. 3rd ed. Harlow, England: Addison Wesley Longman, Inc., 2000.

Pensky, Max. "Migration and Solidarity: Studies in Immigration Law and Policy." MS 2002.

Rawls, John. *The Law of Peoples*. Cambridge, Massachusetts: Harvard University Press, 2001.

Rockefeller, Steven C. "Comment." *Multiculturalism: Examining the Politics of Recognition*. Ed. Amy Gutmann. Princeton, New Jersey: Princeton University Press, 1994. 87-98.

Sen, Amartya. *Development as Freedom*. New York, New York: Anchor Books, 2000.

Statute of the International Courts of Justice. Online. Available
http://icj-cij.org/icjwww/basicdocuments/Basetext/istatute.htm

Taylor, Charles. "The Politics of Recognition." *Multiculturalism: Examining the Politics of Recognition*. Ed. Amy Gutmann. Princeton, New Jersey: Princeton University Press, 1994. 25-73.

Tooze, Roger. "International Political Economy in an Age of Globalization." *The Globalization of World Politics: An Introduction to International Relations*. Ed. John Baylis and Steve Smith. Oxford, England: Oxford University Press, 1999. 212-230.

United Nations Charter. Online. Available http://un.org/aboutun/charter/index.html

United Nations Global Compact. Online. Available
http://www.unglobalcompact.org/un/gc/unweb.nsf/content/whatitis.htm

United Nations Universal Declaration of Human Rights. Online. Available
http://www.un.org./Overview/rights/html

Vincent, R.J. *Human Rights and International Relations*. Cambridge, England: Cambridge University Press, 1986.

Walzer, Michael. "Comment." *Multiculturalism: Examining the Politics of Recognition*. Ed. Amy Gutmann. Princeton, New Jersey: Princeton University Press, 1994. 99-103.

Abstract

Eighty-three years after Wesley Hohfeld published his *Fundamental Legal Conceptions,* the legal right remains largely undefined. Questions regarding the nature and function of the legal right remain unanswered since we lack an appropriate model.

The failure of traditional legal rights models results from the conceptually misleading 'form follows function' methodology adopted by the theorists. In other words, contemporary theorists structure the legal rights model to support their conception of what a legal right ought to do. They analyze the legal right in a vacuum of subjectivity instead of in the context of law. Consequently, traditional models ignore the existence conditions for the development of a legal right.

Rather than defining an arrangement of legal positions and presupposing a normative function, this thesis introduces a new legal rights model titled *Enforced Relation.* This model derives from a general theory of the nature and function of laws and describes an end-state legal relation.

ENFORCED RELATION

Modeling the Legal Right

Thomas Loor Wynn

I. Introduction

> It is all that can be expected if each one of us succeeds in adding a few stones...to the ever-growing edifice which science is rearing. It follows that anything which one writes must largely be made up of a restatement of what has already been said... Each one of us may congratulate himself if he has added something of value, even if that consists only in so rearranging the data which others have accumulated... (Hohfeld 1919: 5)

Walter Cook wrote this passage as part of his introduction to Wesley Hohfeld's *Fundamental Legal Conceptions* (1919). This powerful analogy compares the science of law to a single edifice of intellectual thought and achievement, grounded always in common foundation.

However, it is my contention that the current legal rights models are, for this reason, insufficient.

Traditional legal rights theorists support the conception of a legal right as something that is always positive, whose possession is advantageous. Contemporary models always distinguish between the subject and object of a legal right and protect the right-holder.

I believe the failing of contemporary legal rights theorists follows from their approach. H.L.A. Hart (1973) and Carl Wellman (1985), two of the most influential theorists, began with a conception of how a legal right *ought* to function. The resultant model naturally emerged as a fixed arrangement of legal positions designed to support a legal relation that they assign. This 'form follows function' methodology is not only inappropriate but conceptually misleading,

To me, the words of Walter Cook defined the challenge to recommend a new structure of legal thought. It is my intention to do more than restate the tradition and rearrange past argument. Instead of a model as an arrangement of legal positions, the model of *enforced relation* is structured as combinations of law. This thesis concerns the complete reconstruction of the legal rights model.

II. Select Foundation

The development of a legal rights model requires a preliminary conception of a legal right. I begin with the premise that legal rights define relation. For one party to hold a right implicates a second party in some way. As it stands, however, this conception is highly ambiguous. The terms 'legal relation' and 'legal position' require development.

The work of Wesley Hohfeld, in his *Fundamental Legal Conceptions* (1919), provides the precise vocabulary that this thesis demands. Hohfeld offered an exhaustive classification of eight 'fundamental legal conceptions': right; duty; privilege; no-right; power; liability; immunity; disability. All legal positions existed only in defined pairs. Each conception was comprehensible only as it related to its 'correlative,' or relational position. From the set of eight fundamental legal conceptions, Hohfeld defined four foundational sets of legal relations:

- Claim-Duty
- Liberty-No-Claim
- Power-Liability
- Immunity-Disability

This relation of element-correlative is one of logical equivalence. Each position in a given legal relation is logically connected by virtue of being an equivalent description of the same relation.

The legal positions of a legal privilege, legal right, and legal no-right dictate what is required, forbidden, or permitted. This follows from their logical connection to a legal duty defined as a prescription or prohibition on action. The correlative position to a legal duty is a legal right; the absence of a relational duty is a legal privilege; the opposite of a legal duty is a legal no-right.

The legal positions of a legal liability, legal disability, and legal immunity dictate what was possible or impossible. This follows from their logical connection to a legal power defined as an ability conferred by law to effect some legal relation. The correlative position of a legal power is a legal liability; the absence of a legal power is a legal immunity; the opposite of a legal power is a legal disability.

Before proceeding, I require two substitutions of Hohfeld's original terminology. The substitutions are purely cosmetic, designed only to avoid confusion. Hohfeld included the term 'right' as one of his legal conceptions. Given the purpose of this thesis, I restrict the usage of this term, and substitute the word 'claim' as a "synonym." (Hohfeld, 1919: 38). Secondly, I substitute the word 'liberty' for Hohfeld's fundamental legal conception termed 'privilege.' The term 'privilege' is used widely in an illustration I develop later in this thesis. The substitution of this term, like that of claim for right, in no way alters Hohfeld's assigned meanings.

The dimension of *scope* within the legal relation warrants further consideration. Feinberg (1973), specifically, provides instructive criticism. He draws on the fact that some legal relations are:

> Not "owed" to other persons, but rather to some wholly impersonal authority like "the law" or a painted stop sign. (1973: 63).

To account for this insight, I expand Hohfeld's notion of a legal position to include any legal entity. A legal entity, for the purposes of this thesis, includes any individual, group of individuals, or collective organization. Returning to Feinberg's example, the individual has a duty to stop because the government holds a corresponding claim that obligates the motorist to stop.

This expanded notion of scope also serves to resolve questions of relations involving third parties. Hohfeld has often been read to "assume...that every simple legal position is a jural relation between two and only two natural persons under the law." (Wellman, 1985: 21).

It is my further contention that all legal relations may be ***reduced*** to relations between two legal entities. For example, U.S. citizens have a legal duty to file taxes with the federal government. As a citizen, I am legally obligated to file taxes in virtue of the government's legal claim to a portion of my earnings. Suppose I hire a tax attorney to review and file my taxes. This individual becomes a third party to the initial claim-duty relation. Upon hiring this individual, I exercise a power over him to file my taxes. By virtue of my exercise of power, the attorney is now liable in the sense that he must file my taxes. To retain the notion of a simple, two-party legal relation, I view this situation, and others like it, from different perspectives. On the broadest level, there is the relation between the government and myself. Even though I hired another individual to file my taxes, the government continues to hold a claim over a portion of my earnings, and I remain legally obligated for this claim. On a more detailed level, this broad relation exists as two component two-party relations. I hold a power over the tax attorney and the tax attorney is correspondingly liable to my power. Furthermore, the tax attorney has a power to file my taxes and the federal government is liable to his power.

In view of the preceding, I incorporate from Hohfeld the following:

- All legal positions are exhaustively classified under eight fundamental legal conceptions.
- All legal positions are relational.
- All legal relations are exhaustively classified under four foundational sets of legal relations.
- All legal relations exist between two legal entities.

III. General Theory of Laws

The conception of a legal right as a mechanism for the assignment of relational positions is widely accepted in contemporary legal theory. However, Wellman and Hart ignored the existence conditions of legal rights. In 1980, Joseph Raz pointed out the failing among prevalent legal rights models:

> Attempts to investigate the concepts of [legal] rights have neglected the relations between [legal] rights and the laws instituting them, and that this accounts to a considerable extent for the shortcomings of these attempted elucidations of concepts of [legal] rights. (1980: 178).

Though Raz restricts the focus of his own study to analysis of legal systems, his criticism inadvertently illuminates the fundamental precondition for the existence of legal rights. Legal rights emerge from law and law exists only in the context of a legal system. The only legal rights that exist are those conferred by law. Therefore, if the existence of a legal system is assumed, the appropriate model of a legal right must be founded on a general theory of the function and structure of laws. The appropriate model of a legal right should follow from its conception as a derivative product of law.

While this logic may not seem worthy of mention, the fact of the matter is that current models of legal rights ignore this logical progression. The relation that exists between legal rights and law is one of logical necessity. The criticism offered by Raz is central to the derivation of a new legal rights model. This thesis is designed to bridge the gap between the relational concept of a legal right and its derivation as a product of law.

In the interest of completeness, I begin at the level of the legal system. In many respects, this specification will be unnecessary. However, the following discussion concerns the sources of legal rules, and anyone familiar with the major differences among international legal systems will understand the pains taken to focus this analysis. Therefore, for the purposes of this investigation, I assume the existence of the United States legal system.

Within our legal system, there exist two primary sources of law: statute and precedent. (Post, 1963). The former emerges from legislation passed in Congress; the latter through case law in the judicial branch. Given the working premise of a legal right, the only relevant categories of law are those that relate to the institution of legal positions.

Raz (1980) offers an insightful classification of laws yet certain conclusions are premature. According to Raz, three categories of laws "institute rights." (1980: 178). Investitive laws stipulate the necessary conditions for a subject to acquire a certain legal right. Divestitive laws determine that if a subject holds a certain legal right, and further conditions obtain, the subject loses this legal right. Constitutive laws determine that if a subject holds a certain legal right, and further conditions obtain, the subject holds certain other rights.

The point I wish to make is extremely critical, yet subtle, to this endeavor. Raz stated that legal rights emerge from three types of laws. He then *defines* these types of law in terms of how a legal right is acquired, disposed of, or received in virtue of holding an additional right. Take a moment to consider his logical failing. One cannot define the function of a law in terms of that which it presumably creates or effects. He presents a logically circular argument. The analysis cannot proceed if I accept both the definition of law *in terms of* a legal right and the conception of a law as the precondition for a legal right.

To complete the progression from law to legal right, laws must specify an intermediary step. From the working premise of a legal right as established relation, it logically follows that laws specify legal *positions*. This specification modifies the three categories of law as follows:

- Investitive laws stipulate the necessary conditions for a subject to acquire a certain legal *position*.
- Divestitive laws determine that if a subject holds a certain legal *position*, and further conditions obtain, the subject loses this legal *position*.
- Constitutive laws determine that if a subject holds a certain legal *position*, and further conditions obtain, the subject holds certain other legal *positions*.

IV. Enforced Relation

Starting from a concise restatement of the working premise of a legal right, I proceed to analyze investitive, divestitive, and constitutive laws in isolation and in combination.

The following conditions hold true from the working conception of a legal right:

- A legal right is a relation under law.

- A legal relation consists of legal positions.

Therefore, only laws that confer legal positions are relevant to the institution of rights.

Given the necessary progression for the development of a legal right, it is my contention that the model of a legal right is coherent only as arrangements of law that establish legal positions. The model of *enforced relation* does not define a particular structure of legal relations nor does it presuppose the importance of any legal position. Rather, this model will focus on basic combinations of law that logically produce legal rights. In this model, the term legal right describes an end-state where a legal relation exists under law and cannot be extinguished.

Returning to the categories of law, it should be clear that only investitive law and constitutive law stipulate how a legal position is acquired. A divestitive law, by definition, determines that if a subject holds a certain legal position, and further conditions obtain, the subject loses this legal position. Divestitive laws do not have the mechanism to confer legal position, and therefore, cannot institute legal rights. Investitive laws always exist prior to divestitive laws. Clearly, if there is no law specifying how one may acquire a certain legal position, there cannot exist a law that dictates how that legal position may be disposed of. Finally, not every legal position may be extinguished. In other words, a divestitive law may not always exist in every situation.

Constitutive laws determine how a subject acquires a legal position, provided that the subject holds a certain legal position. By definition, constitutive laws are derivative to investitive laws. For example, the acquisition of a legal position as the legal owner over a piece of property simultaneously confers power to the owner to prosecute trespassers. Investitive law dictates how one acquires this legal claim and constitutive law confers to the subject the additional element of a legal power. I do not dispute the fact that constitutive laws perhaps enhance given legal positions. However, their existence is not fundamental to the model of a legal right. For the purposes of this thesis I exclude consideration of constitutive laws.

Investitive laws are logically prior to divestitive laws and constitutive laws. Therefore, every legal right will necessarily have an investitive law at its foundation. Investitive laws dictate how a legal entity may acquire a relational legal position. If there exists only a single investitive law and no divestitive law, the acquired legal positions emerge as *enforced relation*. The most simple model of a legal right, therefore, is that of a single investitive law.

The notion of an *enforced relation*, as I intend its usage, is best understood through a hypothetical. Imagine a legal system where there exist only investitive laws. All laws, therefore, specify how one acquires legal positions and nothing more. Within this system, any legal position acquired creates a legal relation either of claim-duty; power-liability; liberty-no-claim; or immunity-disability. Now consider what this system lacks. Without divestitive laws, acquired legal positions may not be disposed of, or altered in any way. All legal relations are enforced.

The term enforced is far less important than the recognition of the concept for which the name is sought. For a relation to be enforced indicates that there exists no further mechanism for the disposal of a particular legal relation. The term enforced has nothing to do with consideration of punishment, accusation, compulsion, or the like. It refers only to the situation where an acquired legal position is not disposable by any means. Each party to an *enforced relation* acquires a legal right.

The notion of a legal system of pure investitive law (no divestitive) is of little use beyond select illustrative value. Though pure investitive law exists as a matter of fact, this type of law does not wholly exhaust the system of legal rules. Indeed, countless laws are combinations of all three categories of law. However, just as Hohfeld sought to reduce all legal conceptions to a foundational set, it is my intention to show that legal rights emerge from two foundational combinations of investitive law and divestitive law:

- Single investitive law with no divestitive law
- Single investitive law with a single divestitive law

Recall that all divestitive laws function to extinguish legal relation. However, divestitive laws apply only if specified conditions obtain. Therefore, while divestitive laws exist, certain conditions must obtain for their applicability. Beyond application, divestitive laws exist as two distinct types:

- *Circumstance* Divestitive
- *Choice* Divestitive

A 'circumstance divestitive' law extinguishes the legal relation to which it applies given the facts of the case. A 'choice divestitive' law confers on the subject the *option* of extinguishing a legal position. For clarification purposes, the following illustrations convey the distinction between the combinations of law. The examples proceed in the following order:

- Single investitive law with no divestitive law.
- Single investitive law with a circumstance divestitive law.
- Single investitive law with a choice divestitive law.

V. No Divestitive

Miranda v. Arizona, 384 U.S. 436 (1966) (Miranda) requires the arresting officer to read the 'Warnings of Rights' (Warnings) to any detained subject once he/ she becomes a suspect.

- *Structure*. This precedent follows the model of a single investitive law with no divestitive law.
- *Investitive Conditions.* If an individual is detained and declared a suspect he/ she acquires a legal claim to have their Warnings read. Correspondingly, the law enforcement agents have a legal duty to read the Warnings.
- *Divestitive Conditions.* None.
- *Enforced Relation*. Without a divestitive law to determine how a

legal position may be extinguished, the acquired legal positions, become legally enforced. Therefore, if a suspect is detained, both the arresting officer and the suspect acquire legal rights. The arresting officer holds a legal right to read the Warnings, and the detained suspect holds a legal right to have them read. This relation is enforced under established precedent.

VI. Circumstance Divestitive

Wyatt v. United States, 362 U.S. 525, 528 (1960) upheld spousal privilege as a "rule which bars the testimony of one spouse against the other..." unless the crime committed is against the spouse.[1]

- *Structure.* This precedent follows the model of a single investitive law and a single divestitive law.
- *Investitive Conditions.* If two subjects are legally married, and one spouse is accused of a crime, the other spouse is legally disabled from testifying. Accordingly, the accused spouse is legally immune from his/ her partner's testimony.
- *Divestitive Conditions.* If the crime committed by one spouse is against the other, then the relation of disability-immunity established under investitive law is extinguished. The conditions under which an acquired legal position may be divested depends solely only the facts of the case, and not individual choice.
- *Enforced Relation.*

If the crime committed by one spouse is not against the other, then the relation of immunity-disability, respectively, cannot be extinguished. The divestitive law is inapplicable, and therefore, the legal positions acquired under the investitive law are legally enforced. The spouse of the accused holds a legal right not to testify, and the spouse brought up on charges holds a legal right against his/ her partner's testimony.

If the crime committed by one spouse is in fact against the other, then the relation of immunity-disability acquired under investitive law is automatically extinguished. The spouse against whom the crime was committed is no longer disabled from testifying, and the accused spouse is no longer immune from the other's testimony. As all legal positions are relational, the divestiture of a legal position divests the complete legal relation.

The question follows: If the spouse is no longer legally disabled, and the accused no longer legally immune, what legal relations persist following the divestiture? The notion of a Hohfeldian opposite is the key to establishing the new legal relation. The foundational logic of Hohfeld's matrix (shown below), dictates that to extinguish one's legal relation is to necessarily create another. Specifically, the legal relation created is the opposite of the one extinguished. Hohfeldian opposites are logical contradictories with the same subject. In other words,

> While the existence of one jural correlative logically implies the existence of its correlative legal position, the existence of a jural opposite logically implies the nonexistence of its opposed legal position. (Wellman, 1985: 14).

Elements	Correlatives	Opposites
Claim	Duty	No-Claim
Liberty	No-Claim	Duty
Power	Liability	Disability
Immunity	Disability	Liability

If a legal immunity is divested, the individual automatically acquires the opposite legal position. Following Hohfeld's matrix, the opposite of a legal immunity is a legal liability. Similarly, the opposite of a legal disability is a legal power. The new relation that emerges is therefore one of power-liability. The spouse of the accused now has legal power to testify, and the accused is now liable to the testimony of his/her partner. If there exists no further mechanism for the divestiture of these legal positions, the power-liability relation becomes an *enforced relation*. Accordingly, the spouse of the accused holds a legal *right* to testify and the accused holds a legal *right* to fall subject to this testimony.

VII. Choice Divestitive

The Fifth Amendment of the United States Constitution stipulates: "[No person] shall be compelled in any criminal case to be a witness against himself." This clause protects the accused against self-incriminating testimony.

- *Structure.* This statute follows the model of single investitive law and single divestitive law.
- *Investitive Conditions.* In a criminal case, the accused acquires a legal immunity against self-incriminating testimony. The accused acquires this right by no direct action of his own, but merely by his standing as the accused. Accordingly, this immunity confers a corresponding legal disability on the prosecution to compel testimony.
- *Divestitive Conditions.* The accused may divest this immunity simply by choosing to make statements. While the individual "shall not be compelled," he may divest this immunity by knowingly making statements that may incriminate himself or herself.
- *Enforced Relations.*

If the accused chooses not to dispose of this acquired immunity, the initial relation of immunity-disability remains. It is only following the decision *not* to dispose of tbe legal immunity, and consequently maintain the prosecutor's legal disability, does each party acquire a legal right.

If the accused makes the choice to divest this immunity by knowingly making statements that may incriminate himself or herself, the immunity-disability relation is extinguished. Upon divesting this immunity, and extinguishing the disability on the part of the state, the legal relation becomes one of liability-power. The accused, once immune, is now legally *liable* to the state; the state, previously disabled, holds a legal *power*. If this new relation of power-liability cannot be extinguished, each party acquires a legal right for the legal positions are now enforced under law. The accused exercises the legal *right* to make statements and the state acquires the *right* to use the testimony in a court of law.

VIII. Laws and Legal Rights

The model of *enforced relation* pertains exclusively to *legal* rights. The focus of this thesis is the development of the legal rights model. Underlying the model of enforced relation is the supposition that the existence of the *legal* right requires the precondition of certain laws. This theory, while not discussing their existence or importance, does not discuss human rights. The source of laws, whether natural or man-made, is unimportant. What is important here is the categories of law – investitive, divestitive, and constitutive. Only combinations of these create legal rights.

During the Philosophy, Politics, and Law Honors Conference, panelist Owen Pell, Esq., in pertinent part, asserted that the Miranda and Wyatt United States Supreme Court cases served only to protect basic human rights that existed prior to these decisions.

No one, except an absolute moral skeptic, disputes the existence of human, or fundamental rights prior to Miranda and Wyatt. As stated above, the source of the law is completely irrelevant to this discussion – a point that was unfortunately lost on Mr. Pell. The value of the Miranda and Wyatt cases is the law created by each case and the consequent legal rights – neither of which existed prior to these decisions.

IX. Traditional Models

Legal Advantage. Hohfeld defined an exhaustive set of fundamental legal relations, and concluded that a right, in the strictest sense, was a fundamental relation between two individuals. Only the individual to whom a correlative duty was owed holds a 'legal right.' The matrix of legal conceptions was intended to remove the conceptual confusion surrounding the term 'right,' thereby restricting the term to a single legal advantage. To refer to any other legal advantage (liberty/ immunity/ power) would constitute a "looseness of usage." (Hohfeld 1919: 36).

Hohfeld defined a legal 'right' as one of the *fundamental* legal conceptions. Recall, the conceptions were *sui generis.* Therefore, his rights model is structurally simple, consisting always of a single claim vested in a subject, and a correlative duty vested in another. Given the breadth of this conclusion, Hohfeld offered a wholly inadequate defense. He defended his model with appeal to the proper, ordinary usage of the term 'right':

> ...It is certain that even those who use the word and the conception "right" in the broadest possible way are accustomed to thinking of a "duty" as the invariable correlative. (Hohfeld 1919: 38).

This model of a legal right as a simple claim and correlative duty continues to be the target of extensive criticism by contemporary legal rights theorists. Consider this attack by Honore:

> The right to [money] under the contract may be identical with a claim for the [money] against the debtor. But even this is plausible only as a description of the momentary position of the right-holder. Since there are rules of law by which the duties under contracts are transferred on death...the right to the [money] under the contract remains but the claim securing it is not now against the debtor but against his trustee...(1960: 456-7).

Though Hohfeld's contributions to analytical jurisprudence remain immeasurable, his conclusions regarding the nature and function of legal rights appear premature.

Protected Choice. One of the most widely accepted models is that of protected choice developed by H.L.A. Hart. (1973: 125-148). Every legal right, according to Hart, could be modeled as a core liberty protected by duties to non-interference. That is, every legal right was essentially a liberty *to do*, or *not do,* some particular action. On this view, the legal right functioned to protect autonomy. His paradigm example described a man looking over his garden fence at his neighbor. The man held a legally protected liberty to look or not look at his neighbor. The law obligated the neighbor not to jump the fence and assault his tormentor.

While the intuitive appeal of this model is undisputed, Hart himself conceded that this model was insufficient to account for duties and rights conferred by criminal law. He therefore restricted the applicability of his theory to the realm of "ordinary law." (1973: 146). Wellman (1985) has urged further concessions on the grounds of a conceptually inconsistent standing of legal power in Hart's model. He proceeded to show Hart's theory inadequate to explain the nature of an immunity-right.

To illustrate the inadequacy of protected choice in the realm of criminal law, consider the following. Does an officer of the law have both a legal liberty to arrest or not arrest a suspected killer. Clearly, in this case there should exist no deliberation. The notion of a liberty is incomprehensible in this situation, or any like it. Without further example, the inadequacy of protected choice should be clear. Legal rights do not all function to protect the choice of the right-holder.

Confrontational Model. Wellman rejected protected choice on essentially the same grounds that Hart rejected Hohfeld's simple model. Wellman insisted that the concept of a legal right must be more general to account for the full scope of legal rights. However, instead of proposing a paradigm example to present his theory, Wellman emphasized a necessary framework common to all forms of rights. The language of rights, according to Wellman (1985), was understandable only under adversarial circumstances. The notion of a 'right' presupposed some "conflict of wills." (1985: 193) On this view, the legal right functioned to distribute freedom and control to the right-holder. The necessary model of a legal right, then, was not a conception of a legal right as protected choice. Rather, the appropriate model, according to Wellman, was a confrontational model of distribution.

With minor modification, Wellman's model was structured *exactly* as Hart's. However, instead of a central bilateral liberty, Wellman stated that any legal advantage could serve as the core element. This core advantage was logically central to the integrity of the complete structure because it defined content and scope. To change the core element of legal right changed the right itself.

Surrounding the core element were nested layers of 'associated elements' that comprised the 'periphery.' This 'periphery' was analogous to Hart's 'protective perimeter.' Just as the duties to non-interference served to protect a bilateral liberty in Hart's model, the 'associated elements' in Wellman's model served to confer freedom and control to the right-holder. Since only elements that enhance the core advantage could make up the periphery, it followed that all associated elements were themselves legal advantages. Consequently, Wellman's model of a legal right was a unified system of legal advantages.

On this view, legal positions that do not advantage the right-holder could not be legal rights. This model is unacceptable for the simple fact that some legal rights are necessarily burdens.

X. Developing a New Model

While the legal rights models proposed by Hohfeld, Hart, and Wellman were conceptually distinct regarding the structure and function of a legal right, there was a commonality among all three. Hohfeld, Hart, and Wellman modeled the legal right in terms of defined positions and relations. Hohfeld dictated that a legal right was strictly the correlative of a legal obligation. Hart modeled the legal right as a bilateral liberty with peripheral duties to noninterference. Wellman's model mirrored Hart's structure.

In addition to structuring the legal right in terms of a fixed placement of elements, it appears each model was tailored to fit some preconceived function of a legal right. Instead of identifying and understanding the laws from which legal rights emerge, Hohfeld, Hart, and Wellman modeled the legal right from personal notions of how a legal right ought to function. According to Hohfeld, legal rights functioned to impose legal obligation on a second party. The function of legal rights, following from protected choice, was the protection of individual autonomy. Finally, Wellman claimed that legal rights functioned to confer freedom and control, or "dominion" (1985: 195) to the right-holder.

With the highest level of deference extended to each of my contemporaries, I offer the following analogy. I intend only to highlight the value of my approach regarding the development of an appropriate legal rights model.

Consider Ptolemy's geocentric model of the solar system. Without sophisticated means of analysis, this model was derived primarily through observation. From empirical fact and preconceived (religious) notions of human worth, it was assumed that the universe literally revolved around the Earth. Just as Ptolemy structured the model to fit the conception, contemporary legal rights theorists developed models following a similar destructive pattern. The model of a legal right was arranged to fit a presupposed normative function of legal rights. The geocentric model of the universe, the model of protected choice, and the confrontational model of distribution were all developed without consideration to foundational laws.

The model of *enforced relation* does not presuppose a specific function nor a particular structure of legal positions. The conception of a legal right as *enforced relation* follows logically from an analysis of the laws that establish legal relation. Accordingly, the legal rights models are structured in terms of combinations of laws. Just as the true model of our solar system cannot be described in terms of Pluto, for instance, the model of legal rights cannot be described in terms of any element, or single relation, or even combination of relations. What governs the model of *any* solar system is an understanding of the laws that govern movement and creation. Our particular solar system is merely one possible outcome. Accordingly, the legal right is modeled in terms of those rules that govern its existence. Just as there exists an infinite amount of solar systems, the legal right may itself take infinite forms. The development of a more accurate model comes only with an understanding of the relevant laws. The value to this thesis lies in its appreciation of the existence conditions for legal rights.

As a final recapitulation, the appropriate model of the legal right requires an understanding of the general theory of laws that operate to create, and possibly dispose of, legal relations. The model should not assign a necessary function nor should it attempt to order legal positions to fit some conception. The structure of the elements within the model should be derived from the rules that govern their existence. An appropriate model of a legal right begins with the understanding that laws contain no mechanism for discerning whether legal rights are always 'advantageous' to every right-holder; or whether they confer freedom and control to every right-holder; or whether they protect the individual autonomy of every right-holder. The model of enforced relation begins with an understanding that laws contain no mechanism for discerning whether legal rights protect choice or advantage every right holder. Therefore, it is erroneous to assume that a legal right, as a derivate product of law, will attend to these considerations.

Notes:

1 The exception to spousal privilege has since been expanded to include crimes against the spouse's property, see *Herman v. United States,* 220 F.2d 219,226 (C.A.4 1955). More recently the privilege has been expanded still to include crimes against children of either spouse, see *United States v Allery*, 526 F.2d 1362 (C.A.8 1975).

* Mom, I owe everything to you. You were there with the Conscience Book and you're here now with *Enforced Relation.* I always try to make you proud. I love you. Dad, your mastery of the English language and wealth of knowledge is truly inspiring. Thank you for the thoughtful criticisms and continued guidance. I love you.
Steve, your guidance these past few months have been invaluable. I will remember always that you made this experience possible.

Bibliography

Feinberg, Joel. (1973). *Social Philosophy.* New Jersey: Prentice Hall.

Hart, H.L.A. (1973). "Bentham on Legal Rights." In D. Lyons (ed.) Rights. California: Wadsworth Publishing Company, 125-148.

Hohfeld, Wesley. (1919). *Fundamental Legal Conceptions.* New Haven: Yale University Press.

Post, Gordon. (1963). "Stare Decisis: The Use of Precedent." In J. Arthur and W. Shaw (eds.) Readings in the Philosophy of Law. New Jersey: Prentice Hall, 81-90.

Raz, Joseph. (1980). *The Concept of a Legal System.* Oxford: Clarendon Press.

Wellman, Carl. (1985). *A Theory of Rights.* New Jersey: Rowman & Allenheld Publishers.

Philosophy, Politics and Law

at Binghamton University

PPL Undergraduate Honors Conference

Features six PPL majors who have worked on Honors Projects with philosophy faculty over the past academic year. Each student will deliver a 15 minute presentation and answer questions from the audience and a panel of judges. There will be frequent breaks, so students, faculty, staff, and friends are invited to attend any or all of the talks throughout the evening.

Schedule of Events

3:20	*Introduction*	
3:30 - 4:15	**Adam Ross `02**	"Safety First: Justifying Guaranteed Subsistence Regardless of Responsibility"
4:20 - 5:05	**Gregory Sutton `02**	"Inheritance and Distributive Justice: An Interpretive Pluralist Account"
5:10 - 5:55	**Anna Feigenbaum `02**	"Deliberative Democracy and the Importance of Fostering Dialogical Relationships"
6:00 - 6:30	*Buffet Dinner*	
6:35 - 7:20	**Jonathan Turbin `02**	"State v. the Big Bad Wolf: An Analysis of the Legal Treatment of Rape"
7:25 - 8:10	**Rachel Baskin `02**	"Examining the Relationship Between Globalization and Human Rights"
8:15 - 9:00	**Thomas Wynn `03**	"Enforced Relation: Modeling the Legal Right"
9:15	*Awards Ceremony*	

The Program in Philosophy, Politics and Law offers a diverse liberal arts education which includes core courses in philosophy and complimentary courses in history, political science, economics, and other humanities and social sciences. The major leads to an interdisciplinary B.A. degree offered through Harpur College of Arts and Sciences. PPL also offers a competitive M.A. degree through its combined five-year B.A. / M.A. program. The PPL major provides a foundation for business, teaching, and public service careers, preparation for law and further graduate study.

Special thanks to Professors Tony Preus and John Arthur and alumnus Owen C. Pell, Esq. `80 for serving as panelists in this year's competition. Honors Project directors are Professors Bat-Ami Bar On, Max Pensky, Christopher Knapp, and Steven Scalet. The conference is organized by Professor Scalet and made possible by generous support from Mr. Pell, the Philosophy Department, and the PPL Program.

Binghamton University
Anderson Center Reception Room
Anderson Center
April 29, 2002
3:20 p.m. - 9:00 p.m.
Buffet Dinner at 6:00 p.m.

For conference information, contact Professor Scalet at sscalet@binghamton.edu.

Learn more about PPL at Binghamton at http://ppl.binghamton.edu

ABOUT THE CONTRIBUTORS

Adam Ross received his B.A. in Philosophy, Politics and Law at Binghamton University, The State University of New York. He will begin his work toward a J.D. at Cornell University Law School in the fall. Mr. Ross is currently working on a paper further exploring the connection between safety and freedom.

Gregory Sutton received his B.A. in Philosophy, Politics, and Law from Binghamton University. He will begin graduate studies in law next fall. He is currently working on a paper in law and economics.

Anna Feigenbaum earned her B.A. in Philosophy, Politics, & Law and B.A. in Philosophy from Binghamton University in 2002. Next year she will be pursing a Master's degree in Culture and Communication at the University of East Anglia in Norwich, England.

Jonathan Turbin received his BA in Philosophy, Politics, and Law from Binghamton University. After a brief haitus, he will pursue his graduate studies in public policy/international relations. Mr. Turbin anticipates that his next paper will contrast the legal treatment of homosexuality during the height of the Roman Republic and the Roman Empire under the Caesarian dynast

Rachel Baskin received a B.A. in Philosophy, Politics and Law at Binghamton University and will begin law school in the fall at Benjamin N. Cardozo School of Law. She hopes to continue her studies in international law and immigration, and hopes to write more on both subjects.

Thomas Loor Wynn is currently working toward a Bachelor of Arts in Economics and Philosophy, Politics, and Law from Binghamton University. Next Fall, he will begin research-design for the JC Lui Honors Thesis in Economics. Thomas is also writing a book that outlines a securities trading strategy for intra-day scalping, titled, "Stating the Obvious: Profiting in an Emotionally Directed Environment."